Family Law in Practice
A Study of Cases in the Circuit Court

Family Law in Practice
A Study of Cases in the Circuit Court

By
Carol Coulter

CLARUS PRESS

Published by
Clarus Press Ltd,
Griffith Campus,
South Circular Road,
Dublin 8.

Typeset by
Compuscript Ltd,
Bay 11a, Shannon Industrial Estate
Shannon, Co Clare.

Printed by
Colour Books
Baldoyle, Dublin 13

ISBN
978-1-905536-22-1

Disclaimer
Whilst every effort has been made to ensure that the contents of this book are
accurate, neither the publisher nor author can accept responsibility for any errors
or omissions or loss occasioned to any person acting or refraining from acting as
result of any material in this publication.

CONTENTS

FOREWORD

Family Law in Practice is the welcome fruit of the year spent by Carol Coulter in undertaking the Family Law Reporting Pilot Project, a project established by the Courts Service as a result of the enactment of Section 40 of the Civil Liability and Courts Act 2004. Prior to that change in the law, reporting on the family law courts and research into their day to day practice was rendered virtually impossible by the operation of the *in camera* rule. The only information available was contained in the relatively few reported judgments of the High and Supreme Courts, which dealt in the main with cases where either complex points of law or very high levels of assets were concerned.

While the *in camera* rule operated as a matter of practice with at least a theoretical level of discretion from the foundation of the State, it has been reinforced through its imposition on a mandatory basis in all major family law statutes since the Judicial Separation and Family Law Reform Act 1989. In her Introduction Dr. Coulter rightly highlights the resulting lack of basic information of all kinds concerning an area of law which is of particular interest to the public, touching as it does on aspects of the personal life of the majority of the people.

Writing in 1990 in his Foreword to Duncan and Scully's *Marriage Breakdown in Ireland,* the then President of the Law Reform Commission, and subsequently Chief Justice, Mr. Justice Ronan Keane, commented on family law:

> "Irish law in these areas is a confusing mixture, some of it Victorian and deriving ultimately from the medieval jurisdiction of the 'courts Christian', some of it representing the tentative essays in reform by the modern Irish legislator, some of it reflecting the influence in this area of the Constitution, sometimes baneful, occasionally ambiguous and rarely positive, and a great deal of it the fruits of the judges' struggle to make sense of the whole."

The continuing operation of the *in camera* rule has meant that, despite considerable Constitutional and statutory change since 1990, his remarks still carry weight. Both factual research and jurisprudential analysis have been handicapped by the secrecy enforced by statute.

The public view of the family law courts has been coloured by rumour, hearsay and media commentary, much of it ill-informed and at least in some cases coloured by the personal prejudices of the writer. Those of us who worked on a daily basis in the family law courts found it hard to believe that some of this commentary and public perception bore any relationship whatever to the realities of family law practice. The enactment of Section 40 of the 2004 Act was therefore widely welcomed; at least some limited light could be thrown on courts which had been painted in lurid colours as species of star chambers, if not the equivalent of the medieval inquisition. Despite the numerous public outcries there had been for reporting of the family law courts there seemed, however, to be remarkably little interest shown in finding out the reality by doing the actual work of reporting. Applications to the Minister for Justice, Equality and Law Reform under Section 40 virtually dried up.

Carol Coulter was the welcome exception to this surprising apathy, and under the aegis of the Courts Service she planned, led and managed the Family Law Reporting Pilot Project. This has resulted not only in the periodic and final reports of the Pilot Project but also in the publication of this book, which combines her comprehensive factual reporting and research with an incisive review of family law literature in this jurisdiction and contextually in the common law world. The author rightly points out that, while in recent years there have been quite a number of valuable publications in the Irish family law area, these have in the main been comprehensive accounts of legislation and case law. To date, she points out, there has been little by way of analysis and critique of the law itself or comment on how it is working in practice. Among the few analytical or critical works she mentions the 1996 Law Reform Commission *Report on Family Courts* and the *Sixth Report of the Working Group on a Courts Commission (1998)*, both of which criticised the practical short-comings of the court system, and Frank Martin's 1998 essay *Judicial Discretion in Family Law*, which Dr. Coulter analyses in some detail.

The book ends with an outline of the conclusions the author has reached as a result of both her reporting and her research. Her specific recommendations are well worth following up, and are at the time of writing being positively considered by the Court Service Family Law Reporting Project Committee. But it is hard to disagree with Carol Coulter's conclusion that in general the family law system can be seen to have developed in an *ad hoc* manner, with no over-arching philosophy, and no statement of policy from Government as to what the objectives of the system are. The present economic situation unfortunately renders the allocation of resources for reform all the more doubtful.

In this book Dr. Coulter has given valuable service to the understanding of family law, and her pioneering work as a reporter gives a previously unavailable basis of fact to her critical analysis. There is no doubt that this work will be read by those involved in the practice of family law: it is to be hoped that it will also be read by legislators.

Mrs Justice Catherine McGuinness,
President of the Law Reform Commission

PREFACE

The first divorce was granted in Ireland in February 1997 and by 2006 the number of divorced people in the State (including a small number with foreign divorces) stood at almost 60,000. In that year's Census 107,263 people described themselves as separated, of whom a significant number would have had judicial separations. Yet very little is known of what the outcomes are of the almost 6,000 divorce or separation proceedings that are finalised by the courts each year.

What little is known derives from two sources: the written judgments of the High and Supreme Courts that are reported and make their way into the media; and what are essentially anecdotal accounts of family law proceedings, which make their way into public consciousness either through word of mouth or through one of the parties who is dissatisfied with the outcome complaining about it to the media.

Both of these sources are unrepresentative of the vast bulk of family law cases. Those that are decided in the High Court, or appealed to the Supreme Court, almost invariably involve "high net worth" couples, whose assets are valued at many millions of euro. Less than two per cent of all divorces and separations are heard in the High Court. Most couples who separate and divorce have a family home and perhaps some savings or a pension, and little else, so their situation cannot be compared to the typical High Court case. Details of cases where a dissatisfied litigant complains about an outcome to the media are also unrepresentative of the majority of cases for a number of reasons. Not only do most of the, approximately, 12,000 family law litigants who are separated or divorced by the courts each year not complain to the media, those that do represent only one half of the couple involved, and their version of what occurred will inevitably be one-sided.

It is thus impossible for those faced with family law proceedings, and even sometimes their lawyers, to know what to expect. Prospective family law litigants may have unrealistic expectations of family law litigation, or, equally, harbour unwarranted fears.

Further, evidence-based discussion of how family law is operating in Ireland has been extremely difficult. All this has been due to the operation of the *in camera* rule which, until recently, prevented anyone from observing what went on in the family courts. The modifications to this rule introduced by the Civil Liability and Courts Act 2004 permitted a number of categories of people, including academic researchers, to attend court proceedings in order to write reports. While this falls far short of what many commentators, including this writer, sought, it represents a start that hopefully can be expanded.

I was privileged to be able to attend family law proceedings both as a student preparing an M Phil thesis and as the person nominated by the Courts Service to run its pilot project on family law reporting. The material collected during that year, which ran from October 2006 to October 2007, forms the basis of this book.

My primary purpose was to assemble the evidence to permit an informed discussion about how our family law system works, identify its failings and propose remedies. The evidence was drawn from two sources: the written files recording the ancillary orders made in family law cases where divorces and judicial separations were granted; and my notes from my attendance at Circuit Court family law hearings throughout the year. It was then possible to see what patterns emerged in relation to the distribution of assets, the disposal of the family home, the outcome of the case for dependent children, and other issues. It was also possible to see what patterns emerged in judicial decision-making: whether decisions tended to vary widely from one Circuit to another or from one judge to another; whether there appeared to be any bias against any particular category of litigant; whether other factors, like delay and the operation of the legal aid scheme, had an adverse impact on litigants.

The system has many imperfections, as outlined in the final chapter of this book. Some, of an essentially administrative nature, are being addressed by the Courts Service and by the judiciary. Others, particularly the priority given to family law, the need to put children at the centre of family law proceedings, the need for resources to be put into alternatives to court proceedings and to families under stress, the need to reconsider the way our civil legal aid system works, are matters for policy-makers.

The place of the family in our society, how it is defined in the Constitution and the importance of the recognition of children's rights, are all now receiving attention. The role of our family law legislation, an evaluation of how it is working and how it needs to be amended, the role of the courts and how they can provide a better service for people at a very difficult period in their lives, need to be part of this discussion, but a part based on facts rather than on assumptions and anecdotes. I hope this book will play a part in that discussion.

Carol Coulter
10th February 2009

ACKNOWLEDGEMENTS

I wish to acknowledge the support of the *Irish Times* newspaper and in particular of its editor, Geraldine Kennedy, who gave me sabbatical leave and financial support to embark on this work, and a year's leave which enabled me to carry out the research, mainly conducted while engaged in the Courts Service Family Law Reporting Pilot Project. I would like to thank the then Minister for Justice, Michael McDowell SC, for his permission to attend family law proceedings in order to conduct this research initially.

I would like to thank the chief executive of the Courts Service, P J Fitzpatrick, and its board, for permission to use the material obtained while carrying out the pilot project on reporting family law for the Courts Service. Courts Service staff around the country were generous with their help, especially in making sense of family law files, and family lawyers and members of judiciary gave their time to share their experience, views and insights. Luke O'Neill, of the Courts Service media relations service, gave me additional help in obtaining the gender breakdown of the Dublin Circuit Court cases for October 2006 and I would also like to thank Helen Priestly of the Courts Service Information Office for providing the photograph which illustrates the cover of this book.

Tony Cerasi of the *Irish Times* studio provided invaluable assistance in producing the tables in Chapter 2. Fergus Ryan and Geoffrey Shannon were hugely enthusiastic about the project, and gave generously of their time and freely shared their knowledge and expertise.

I would like also to thank David McCartney for his care and professionalism in bringing the book to publication. This book would be the poorer without such assistance and that of many others. Its short-comings, however, are entirely my own.

Finally, I would like to thank Harry Vince, without whose encouragement, advice, support and constant prodding neither this nor many other projects would have been either embarked upon or completed.

INTRODUCTION

All research on law can be used for a number of purposes: to inform legal professionals of developments in the field; to inform policy-makers; to inform the general public; to question aspects of the law and the policy underlying it and to advocate changes in the policy and the law.

All of these purposes can also be served by research on family law. Further, it is an area of particular interest to the public, as it touches on aspects of the intimate and personal life of the majority of people. As family law is concerned not only with the resolution of difficulties when families get into trouble, but with the promotion of the family as "the fundamental unit group of society" (Art 41 of the Irish Constitution), it can be said to concern every citizen.

But, unlike the debate on other aspects of law, debate on family law in Ireland has been limited by a dearth of research on how recent family law works in practice. This is due largely to the *in camera* rule, which prohibited access even from researchers to family law courts, with the only available material those judgments of the superior courts that were reported. This is compounded by the fact that the very existence of family law is a relatively new phenomenon (Duncan, 1978: 19), as well as the fact that records of how it operates are limited to two sources, the aforementioned reported judgments of the superior courts and some very bare statistics produced by the Courts Service in its annual reports (2006: 124–125). The latter tell us how many divorces, judicial separations, barring orders, protection orders and maintenance orders there are on an annual basis, but little else. We have no idea of the social reality behind these statistics, or even what proportion of these orders is sought by women and what by men. The judgments of the High and Supreme Courts, while providing important insights into certain categories of marriage breakdown, and developing the law as laid down in the legislation, are not representative of the vast majority of cases that end up before the courts, as they are overwhelmingly based on cases involving high net worth marital assets or complex issues of law (Durcan, 2007).

While this has meant that there has been limited academic debate about family law policy and its reform in Ireland, it has not deterred commentators in the media from calling for reform. In particular it has been alleged that family law in Ireland, reflecting family law in other jurisdictions, is biased against men in general and fathers in particular (Waters,

Irish Times, August 14, 2006, May 29, 2006, August 15, 2004, November 1, 2004, October 18, 2004, Nov 19, 2001, September 10, 2001, May 13, 1999. This is a representative selection. A search of the *Irish Times* archive for references by John Waters to "family law" and "fathers" produces 46 results). In the absence of any scientific study of judicial decisions, such assertions are impossible either to verify or to refute. It can merely be observed that journalists (this writer included) are the recipients of voluminous correspondence about alleged injustices at the hands of the family law system, and the complainants are by no means only men. By definition, those involved in court cases who are satisfied with the outcome are unlikely to seek to have their situation highlighted in the media. Those who do, therefore, are not a representative selection of all litigants.

For many years, therefore, informed debate on family law was hampered by the *in camera* rule. The only exception was in the High Court when written judgments were handed down and reported, with the parties' names and some (though not necessarily all) identifying details redacted. This meant that the only cases that came into the public domain with all the facts stated clearly (other than cases where one party approached a journalist) were those heard in the High Court which, by definition, were usually "ample resources" cases and therefore not typical.

It is ironic that, while the period running up to the referenda on divorce in 1986 and 1995 saw widespread public discussion of family break-down and the impact of divorce on society, this discussion came to an abrupt end when divorce was introduced. No attempt was made, or could be made, to examine how it was working out in practice while the *in camera* rule remained in place. This situation was criticised by the Law Reform Commission in its 1996 *Report on the Family Courts* (LRC 52-1996: 115).

Reform of the *In Camera* Rule

Ireland has a written Constitution which guarantees the administration of justice in public, except for such exceptional circumstances as may be prescribed by law (Art.34.1), and this must be taken into account in dealing with the interaction between the need to provide information on family law and access to the courts by the media and others (for a fuller discussion on the operation of the *in camera* rule, see Coulter, *Family Law Reporting Pilot Project, Report to the Board of the Courts Service,* 2007: 4–5). Sustained criticism of the rule by members of the judiciary, the Law Reform Commission and the Courts Service (Report of the Family Law Monitoring Committee on the commencement, implementation and development of the Family Law Reporting Service Pilot Project, 2002, unpublished), as well as by commentators (see McCormack, 2000), led to a pledge to reform it in the 2002 Programme for Government (Agreed Programme for Government between Fianna Fáil and the Progressive Democrats, June 2002: 29).

In 2004 the Minister for Justice included, in s 40 of the Civil Liability and Courts Act 2004, provisions for modifying the *in camera* rule in relation to family law. The legislation left the details on who was to have access to family law courts to Regulations to be made later by the Minister. In the Dáil and Seanad debates on the matter it appeared that the availability of information on family law, rather than the exercise of the principle that justice be administered in public, was uppermost in the mind of the legislature (McDowell, 2007).

Having listed the principal Acts enforcing the *in camera* rule as the Family Home Protection Act 1976, the Courts Act 1081, the Judicial Separation and Family Law (Reform) Act 1989, the Courts Act 1991, the Family Law Act 1995 and the Family Law (Divorce) Act 1996, it continues:

"Nothing contained in a relevant enactment shall operate to prohibit –

1   the preparation by a barrister at law or a solicitor or a person falling within any other class of persons specified in regulations made by the Minister and publication of a report of proceedings to which the relevant enactment relates, or

2   the publication of the decision of the court in such proceedings, in accordance with rules of court, provided that the report or decision does not contain any information which would enable the parties to the proceedings or any child to which the proceedings relate to be identified and, accordingly, unless in the special circumstances of the matter the court, for reasons which shall be specified in the direction, otherwise directs, a person referred to in paragraph (a) may, for the purposes of preparing such a report, attend the proceedings subject to any direction the court may give in that behalf."

Thus the only class of person specifically permitted by the legislation to attend family law proceedings and prepare reports is "a barrister-at-law or a solicitor". The type of report a barrister or solicitor might prepare, or for whom, is not specified in the legislation. It therefore seems that there is a *lacuna* in the legislation, unintended by the Oireachtas, whereby a barrister or a solicitor working for the media could prepare reports that would be published in the media. The only protection against this, if such protection is required, is the stipulation in s 40(b) that the publication of a report be "in accordance with rules of court".

The implementation of the Act, therefore, depended on two qualifications, the introduction of Regulations and the adoption by the relevant jurisdictions of Rules of Court.

The Regulations referred to in the Act were made by the Minister in Statutory Instrument (Civil Liability and Courts Act 2004 (s 40(3)) Regulations 2005, SI No. 337 of 2005). Under them, three classes of person other than lawyers could attend family law cases "in order to draw up and publish reports". These included family mediators, persons engaged in family law research and accredited to reputable academic or research institutions, and "persons engaged by the Courts Service to prepare court reports of proceedings".

I was privileged to be chosen by the Courts Service to carry out this work on a pilot basis, and the material I collected during this project forms the basis of this work.

Anonymity of the Parties

A major concern at the outset was the need to preserve the anonymity of the parties, both in accordance with the legislation and for ethical reasons. Accordingly, as part of this project I drew up a Protocol for reporting on family law proceedings which I used on all my reports for the Courts Service, and which is followed in cases described in this work. It is also currently being used by the barristers working for the Courts Service in the continuation of the project. It provides for writing reports in a way that all geographical and professional detail that might lead to the identification of the parties is removed. A copy of it is appended to this work.

The emphasis in Irish legislation is on allowing for more information on the operation of the family courts to be made available to interested bodies and the public, the latter through academic research and the work of the Courts Service. There is little emphasis on the public scrutiny aspect of the administration of justice in public. Taking the Act and the Regulations together, it would appear that it was the intention of the legislature to leave the class of person to be permitted to attend family law proceedings to the discretion of the Minister, perhaps allowing the classes of person be expanded over time, and to include members of the media.

If there is a public demand for media access to the family courts, and if it appears from the Pilot Project and any further development of the project that may be undertaken by the Courts Service, that broader media reporting of family law is possible without jeopardising the privacy of the family, it is open to the Minister to expand the classes of person who attend such proceedings to include *bona fide* members of the media, provided they agree to abide by Rules of Court and any direction the court may give. (See Recommendations in Coulter, 2007: 29–31) Such directions could include detailed instructions on the nature of the information that should be excluded from reports in order to ensure the anonymity of the parties. The fact that a Protocol already exists restricting the information that can be given about parties may provide reassurance in this regard.

Rules of Court

The Rules of Court committees of the three jurisdictions of the courts (District, Circuit and High) drew up Rules of Court that would apply to a person presenting themselves in order to prepare a report. While slightly varying in detail, all of them provided that the person should "prior to or at the commencement of the hearing of the proceedings, identify him or herself to the Court and apply for such directions as the Court may give under Section 40(3) of the said Act." If the Court is satisfied that this person is someone to whom the section applies, "having heard any submission made by or on behalf of any party to the proceedings, [it] may allow the applicant to attend the proceedings subject to such directions as the Court may give in that regard."

The Act provides for those listed to attend family law proceedings, but also gives the Court discretion to exclude them in "the special circumstances of the matter" and for "reasons that shall be stated in the direction". The "special circumstances of the matter" that might lead to a reporter or researcher being excluded from proceedings are nowhere defined, and this probably remains a task for the judiciary itself to clarify through case-law.

The position of academic researchers remains relatively unexplored. I am grateful to the Chief Executive of the Courts Service for his permission, on behalf of the Board, to use the material I collected for it as the basis for this work.

Material
The above, then, forms the legal and regulatory framework under which this research was carried out. It meant that I had unrestricted access to all the family courts in all three jurisdictions and was able to attend and take notes of proceedings. I was also given permission by the Presidents of the three jurisdictions to examine files for the purpose of compiling statistics on family law. It was not possible to attend hearings in all three jurisdictions and, as my focus was on proceedings surrounding marriage breakdown, and as approximately 98.5 percent of all judicial separations and divorces are decided in the Circuit Court (Courts Service Annual Report 2006: 124), the material is drawn from my examination of this jurisdiction.

The material on which this work is based includes notes from my examination of the family law files of all eight Circuit Courts over a given period (see below), and notes taken during my attendance at family law proceedings during the 2006/2007 legal year. I examined both processes and outcomes, but focused on outcomes, in order to assemble a body of data on how family law works out in practice in Ireland. In particular I looked at both orders made by the courts and consents drawn up by the parties in settlement proceedings and made a rule of court, to attempt to discern trends such as: whether men or women were more likely to instigate proceedings; whether marriage breakdown was more prevalent among couples after any specific length of marriage; the proportion of judicial separations and divorces that ended in settlement and the proportion that went to a full court hearing; how marriage breakdown affected children and their parents, particularly with regard to custody, access and maintenance; how the resources of the family were divided; the disposition of the family home; and how matters like relations with other family members and the conduct of the parties impacted on the outcome of family law proceedings.

When looking at the cases I attended in court I considered similar issues to those revealed in the files, such as the ages of the litigants, whether or not they had dependent children and their socio-economic circumstances insofar as this emerged during the case, and the outcomes of the cases. I examined the outcomes under the following main headings: custody of and access to dependent children (if there were any); disposal of the family home; maintenance and other financial reliefs; and the role of conduct in the proceedings and outcome, if there was any. I hoped this would indicate to those in the legal system and to policy makers what the impact of legislation in the area of family law had been and where policy changes or improvements were needed.

My research, which looked at statistics and the impact of the law as well as how the law itself was interpreted, includes sociological as well as legal research, and also includes the input of disciplines like psychology into the overall processes involved in family law. It is therefore an interdisciplinary approach. I have used the Harvard referencing system for all academic references, as is most appropriate to this type of work.

Chapter 1

REVIEW OF LITERATURE AND NOTES ON METHODOLOGY

Critical analysis of family law is a recent discipline, and is more recent in Ireland than elsewhere in the common law world, largely due to the fact that divorce is only a decade old in this jurisdiction. Irish family law exists within the common law tradition, and indeed has its origins in English family law. To this day precedents established by the English higher courts in the area of family law have heavily persuasive value in the Irish courts. Any work on Irish family law, therefore, takes place within a context established by historical, theoretical and analytical work carried out on the basis of the development of family law elsewhere in the common law tradition.

Whether implicitly or explicitly, family law is based on notions of what the family is, and how it is—and can be—shaped by law. There is clearly no unanimity on these questions. Frances Olsen has identified two views of the family, the positivist view and the natural view (1985: 846). The former sees the family as constructed by law; the latter sees it as pre-existing, created by God or nature, and *recognised* by law. This view is that expressed by the Irish Constitution (Art 41.1.1), and judicially endorsed (see Preface by Walsh, J in Binchy, 1984: vi) but it has been modified by a positivist view as family roles and obligations are outlined by statute and the courts (see Martin, 1998: 169). The positivist view has dominated academic writing on marriage and the family outside Ireland. These issues are looked at from a sociological perspective in works like the 1995 collection, *Irish Family Studies: Selected Papers* (McCarthy, 1995).

THE INTERNATIONAL CONTEXT IN THE COMMON LAW WORLD

Early writing on the family and law examined the burgeoning phenomenon of marital breakdown. Jack Dominian drew together work collated from the disciplines of sociology and psychology to outline the changing nature of marriage and the new pressures on it, in *Marital Breakdown*, written in 1968. At that time he was able to write: "The impact of marital breakdown on the family is difficult to assess and so far few studies which have attempted to do this in detail exist." (1968: 118). The same could not be said today. Indeed, 27 years later Dominian was one of the authors of a study for the counselling organisation, One Plus One, which sought to quantify the affects of marital breakdown on the health of the population in the United Kingdom. (McAllister, 1995).

In the United States, J Ross Eshleman does not dwell on philosophy as he attempts to grapple with the nature of the family, specifically the American family, in *The Family, An Introduction* (1984, updated in 1991). Instead he takes a historical and descriptive approach. Outlining the functions it historically performed, he points out that many of these functions (economic, bestowing status, educational, protective, religious, recreational, providing affection) are increasingly being removed from the exclusive domain of the family, which is also affected by the increased participation of women in the workforce (Eshleman: 13). His examination of the different forms the family takes, and the different emphases of its various functions within different cultures, is useful even outside of the United States framework in which it is placed.

Also in the United States, Mary Glendon has outlined the complex interaction between the state, the family and the law in her eponymous work (1977). Four years later she wrote: "The new family is a concept that represents a variety of co-existing family types" (Glendon, 1981: 4), an idea that has been developed by other writers in more detail since. However, her expectation that job-protection and other forms of economic support from outside the family would replace the traditional support given to individuals by the family have proved to be ill-founded as least as far as the small nuclear, as opposed to the extended family, is concerned.

Different ways of understanding the family provide an interesting backdrop to the study of family law, and there can be no conclusive definitions. Some writers do not concern themselves with this question at all, while others consider how the evolution of the law throws into question our notion of what the family is. Much of the work carried out in other common law jurisdictions falls into one of two categories, though they are by no means mutually exclusive and are often contained within the one work: that which describes how the law works; and critiques of the law and the assumptions underlying it. The latter has focussed on how the law has interacted with society and its expectations, and with political policy. It interrogates the whole idea of the family and outlines how the law has attempted, with varying degrees of success, to adapt to its changing contours.

The study of family law as an academic discipline only really began after the Second World War, and one of the first attempts to draw together the different strands is that of Jack Dominian (1968) whose work is now outdated due to changes in the law and in social policy. The law concerning the family in England and Wales underwent major changes in subsequent decades, which have been chronicled and commented upon by writers like Cretney (2003), Dewar and Parker (2003), Diduck and Kaganas (2006), while Carolyn Hamilton and Alison Perry have written a comprehensive comparative work outlining family law across most of the states of Europe, and in the EU itself (Hamilton and Perry, 2002). These works are authoritative statements of the law as it stands and helpful works of reference.

The complex relationship between the family, law and the state has been comprehensively explored by academic commentators in the United States, Britain and Australia, to name three major common law jurisdictions, whose work contain many insights for those studying family law in Ireland.

As well as chronicling family law, Dewar is one of its foremost commentators in the UK and Australia. In a series of works he engages in debate with those viewing it from a functionalist, feminist, familialist or critical theorist perspective (Dewar and Parker, 1992; Dewar, 1996; Dewar, 1998; Dewar and Parker, 2002). He is much preoccupied by the fact that family law seems to evade strictly legal analysis. In his 1998 essay, "The Normal Chaos of Family Law", he writes: "Family law... is contradictory, disordered, incoherent and, in part at least, antinomic," adding that it deals with areas of social life and feeling "that are themselves riven with contradiction or paradox." (1998: 468).

He identifies dangers in the evolution of modern family law, with its growing emphasis on non-judicial solutions. In 1992 he wrote: "There are increasing doubts about abandoning traditional legal conceptions of rights or traditional legal methods of dispute resolution" (1992: 5) and six years later he writes: "Those who negotiate privately are relieved of the burden of justifying their outcomes to anyone other than themselves and perhaps the cursory scrutiny of a judge" (1998: 474).

In a comment that has relevance for Irish family law, he says that the removal of the "fault" criterion as the basis for decision-making in divorce cases left "no clear principle as the basis for decisions. Instead, they were to be dealt with according to utilitarian or consequentialist criteria" (1998: 472). He joins forces again with Stephen Parker to edit a collection of essays published in 2003, which draw together the proceedings of an international conference on family law in Brisbane, Australia, in 2000. This enabled them to identify a number of threads in modern family law, including: the impact of constitutional and human rights norms, and of local cultural or religious norms; post-separation parenting and giving children an effective voice; the diversity of family life; the role of lawyers and the courts, and of specialist interventions; and the ongoing question of the funding of both legal and non-legal services for those involved in relationship re-ordering. These themes could form a useful template for examining the present state of family law in Ireland.

Function of Family Law

John Eekelaar was the first to examine family law from the standpoint of the function it was intended to serve, and his influential book, *Family Law and Social Policy* (1984), continues to inform debate. His comment, "where an institution such as marriage is heavily overladen with legal rules, it is obvious that the lawmakers, at least, desired the institution to further certain objectives", (1984: 16) clearly has wide relevance. When he points out that at the time of divorce the legal system can survey the history of the marriage, weighing and evaluating the contributions made to it by each spouse, and drawing up a balance-sheet; and can also look forward, seeking to anticipate the needs which the parties and their children are likely to face in the new circumstances (1984: 37), he is describing what has actually been outlined in a number of High Court judgments, as has been fully described by Geoffrey Shannon in his latest book, *Divorce Law and Practice* (2007: 74–93). But Eekelaar also warns that these two strands, the balance sheet and provision for the future, may not always be compatible, and suggests that every divorce system can be seen to incline more to the one than the other (1984: 37).

The rest of this work involves a detailed study of what happens in divorce in England and Wales, with reference to US studies, which is valuable to anyone interested in the family and its regulation by the legal system, but it also serves to underline the absence of data on which similar work could be based in Ireland.

Eekelaar's work has faced criticism. O'Donovan points out that his critics "argue that definition and clarity are not entirely achieved" (1993: 19), while Dewar also states that the "functions" are not always unambiguous or obvious (1992: 4). O'Donovan also claims that his method does not concern questions like power within the family, "the privileging of family members on the basis of gender by state agencies, the silence of the subordinated." (1993: 20).

Eekelaar takes account of developments in the debate in family law in the collection he edited with Sanford Katz and Mavis Maclean sixteen years later, *Cross Currents: Family Law and Policy in the US and England* (2000). While restating his position that, "historically, an individual's rights and duties, his or her social role, depends on the individual's relationship to social institutions," he points out that today the individual has emerged as the focus of concern, the driver of policy and the source of rights (2000: 647). While "welfarism" became the dominant theme in family law at the end of the twentieth century, today "empowerment" dominates the rhetoric. However, this is more illusory than real. "The illusion of empowerment is created, while the state keeps control over how the power is exercised" (2000: 649).

The role of the state in the family in a very different political and legal context, that of the United States, is explored by Frances Olsen in a number of publications, including "The Myth of State Intervention in the Family" (1985 a) and "The Family and the Market: A study of Ideology and Legal Reform" (1985 b). However, they only serve to emphasise how distant the ideological debate she engages in is from the current state of debate about the state, the family and the law in Ireland, where this discussion has scarcely begun (see below for a survey of Irish work in the area).

Katherine O'Donovan, M D A Freeman, Alison Diduck and others argue for a close interrogation of the origins of family law and the interests its serves. Setting out his stall for a critical theory of family law Freeman points out, "family law is principally about the state and society" (1985:162). Therefore, he argues, a theory about the extent of the legitimate role of the state in society is necessary. Without a critical theory of family law it is difficult to assess the value of new techniques, practices or institutions (1985: 164). Policies and concepts used in family law like "welfare" and "the best interests of the child" need to be critically examined, he argues, and he suggests that the family has been "colonised" by welfare professionals (1985: 165), a theme taken up by certain Irish commentators (see John Waters's columns in *The Irish Times,* referred to in the Introduction).

In *Law's Families* Diduck writes: "We see ... throughout the history of divorce law reform in general and indeed the history of family law reform in general, a preoccupation with, verging on anxiety about, stable society's dependence upon stable marriages" (2003: 45). Policy has been based on the position that law can be used to influence people's behaviour, and that it should be so used, she writes.

She then traces the history of various reforming initiatives in the UK, and identifies a problem she sees with the growth of the "welfare discourse" in family law. "It implies that relations between children and parents or between intimates do not have to be considered as matters of civil rights, as politically legitimate sites of grievance or as deserving of the authority and protection of the rule of law" (2003: 120). However, she sees a recent change in this context as a political culture of individual rights, influenced by the jurisprudence of the European Court of Human Rights, gains more widespread currency (2003: 199).

The Influence of Feminism

Feminism has clearly influenced these commentators, as it has the work of Carol Smart in *The Ties that Bind* (1984) and John Collier in *Masculinity, Law and the Family* (1995). Later, in *Family Law, Gender and the State: Text, Cases and Materials,* Alison Diduck and Felicity Kaganas offer a very comprehensive evaluation, from a feminist standpoint, of the practice of family law, both past and present, in England and Wales (2006).

Such debates can have a more than theoretical influence. Leonore Weitzman's *The Divorce Revolution* (1985), which argued that a year after a divorce women's standard of living had dropped by 73 percent, while that of men had increased by 43 percent, was, according to critic Richard R Peterson, quoted in 24 legal cases, including one in the US Supreme Court (Peterson, 1996). They were widely used by feminists to argue for increased levels of child support. Her figures were based on a study of 228 couples who divorced in Los Angeles between 1977 and 1978. Dr Peterson obtained access to her data and re-analysed it, finding her figures to be wrong, and he concluded that in fact women's standard of living fell by 27 percent and that of men increased by 10 percent (*op. cit*). Dr Weitzman conceded that her figures were probably wrong because she had "over-sampled" couples who had been in longer marriages and with average or above-average incomes (*New York Times*, 9th May 1996).

A much more comprehensive US study, by Atlee Stroup and Gene Pollock, based on a survey of 7,500 adults between 1983 and 1987, found that everyone experienced a decline in income after divorce, and that men, especially unskilled men, did not benefit financially from divorce (Stroud and Pollock, 1994).

No such study exists for Ireland, and caution must be exercised in drawing parallels between the experience of other legal regimes and cultures and those of Ireland. The conclusion that it is more difficult for two households to be maintained on the resources that previously maintained one, at least in the immediate aftermath of a divorce when no additional resources are in prospect, would appear to be obvious. What these studies show above all is the crucial importance of comprehensive, thorough and accurate empirical research, and the need for the exercise of great caution before basing policy on any single work.

WORK ON IRISH FAMILY LAW

William Duncan can claim to be the pioneer of critical writing on family law in Ireland, and he identified early on the difficulty of comparing it with family law elsewhere. In his 1977 essay, "Supporting the Institution of Marriage in Ireland", he remarks: "It is not easy to fit the history of Irish marriage laws neatly into the tapestry of Western European developments so attractively constructed by Professor Glendon in *State, Law and Family*" (1978: 215/216) and this statement could be replicated today, over 30 years later, in relation to most contemporary commentary on family law.

Referring to the uniqueness of the Irish experience, Duncan points out that none of the legal developments of the nineteenth century had much relevance for the majority of the Irish population, as they concerned the relationship of the state to the ecclesiastical courts of the established church in England. He points out that Catholic marriages were not statutorily provided for until 1870, and then only when the parties were not of the same religious denomination. Thus the context for the development of family law in Ireland was absent.

He writes that in Ireland "since 1870 no significant attempts have been made to establish the authority or relevance of the civil law in matters of matrimonial status" (1978: 219). That state of affairs has clearly changed since he wrote this article in 1978, but most of the major changes have only come in the past 20 years, and his comment illustrates the youthful nature of family law as an academic discipline in Ireland.

Irish commentary so far, with the exception of Fahey and Lyons' seminal work (1995), falls into two categories: that preceding the introduction of divorce through the referendum removing the constitutional ban in 1995 and the enactment of the enabling legislation in 1996, which has examined the reality of marriage breakdown and the attempts to deal with it in the absence of divorce; and that following the removal of the constitutional ban and the subsequent introduction of divorce legislation, which has analysed this and related legislation and the judgments that followed it.

There has, of course, been considerable academic work in the fields of sociology and history on the changing nature of the family in Ireland, but this has generally been divorced from its legal construction. They have come together in the Report of the Constitution Review Group (1996), and report and debates of the Oireachtas Committee on the Constitution (1997), but these have not, so far, been translated into legal definitions that go beyond the constitutional definition of the family.

Pre-1996 Work

Prior to 1996, work on Irish family law was dominated by three commentators, William Duncan, William Binchy and Alan Shatter. Binchy's *Casebook on Irish Family Law* was the first attempt to draw together the jurisprudence to date, and contained an important Preface by Supreme Court judge, Brian Walsh, who outlined the constitutional framework for family law and attempts to reform it. "The family ... does not depend for its existence upon positive law," he writes, "[it is] above all, a moral institution" (1984: vi). He anticipates various reports from expert bodies (Law Reform Commission, 1996; Denham, Sixth Report on a Courts Commission, 1998) when he writes: "There is much to be said for the creation of a unified family court which would be manned by a body of judges drawn from the different judicial levels of our courts", envisaging that such a court would have the assistance of social workers and other professionals as assessors (1984: vii). In general, Binchy's book offers an interesting overview of the attitudes of the courts to family matters up to 1984, but, because it predates so much significant legislation in the area, it is now primarily of historical interest.

Six years later William Duncan and Paula Scully embarked on an ambitious survey of family law in Ireland to date, with chapters on topics such as nullity, barring and protection orders, judicial separation (in the light of the recently enacted Judicial Separation and Family Law Act 1989), maintenance and other financial provisions, child custody and access disputes and separation agreements (1990). Each chapter contains a synopsis of the legal principles involved, and then outlines the practice and procedures that follow. It would have been an invaluable handbook for all practitioners and, indeed, members of the judiciary dealing with family law.

Alan Shatter wrote his first book on family law in 1977, and there have been three editions since, with the fourth published in 1997 after the introduction of divorce. This is a monumental work, dealing with all aspects of family law, including extensive references to case-law. Again, it is an important work of reference. Others, like O'Connor (1988) attempted to synopsise the essential elements in Irish family law, especially for students. The issue of the financial consequences of marriage breakdown is examined by Peter Ward in *Divorce in Ireland, Who should bear the cost?* (1993), written prior to the introduction of divorce.

Fahey and Lyons

Although not a work of legal analysis, the sociological study by Fahey and Lyons has set a benchmark for the study of the operation of family law in Ireland (1995). Written on the eve of the second divorce referendum, it was the first and, so far, only attempt to look behind the bare statistics of the cases going to court to find out what they revealed about the modern Irish family. The authors examined files in solicitors' offices, both private and those working for the Legal Aid Board, and asked the following questions: what are the main types of cases, who are the clients, what issues are they seeking to have addressed, and what are the legal outcomes (1995: 3). Their sample was large—they studied 510 cases from 87 solicitors, and also drew information gleaned from standardised forms filled in by court registrars in Dolphin House, the main court dealing with family law at District Court level. They did not conduct interviews with litigants, though solicitors were interviewed to supplement the information contained in their files. Their research was based on a quantitative, rather than a qualitative methodology, therefore, but was none the less valuable for that.

Through it they were able to conclude that the bulk of family law cases, in the absence of divorce, were able to fall into two categories: those which dealt with protection matters, primarily through protection and barring orders, and those that dealt with legal separations. The majority of legally-aided clients had recourse to the courts for orders relating to protection, while the majority of the clients of private solicitors were seeking legal separations. Both groups of clients also usually sought assistance with financial matters like maintenance and property adjustment, but this was more of a concern to clients seeking legal separations.

The book provided a crucial insight into the reality of marital breakdown in Ireland just as the divorce referendum was being voted upon, and may indeed have affected the outcome, which was the narrowest possible vote in favour of removing the constitutional prohibition. It showed that marital breakdown was a reality, but one that could not be measured by a single legal procedure, like legal separation. Instead, people sought the legal solution most suited to their needs. For people with very limited resources, that solution was the physical separation and safety secured through a barring order. For those with greater material resources, a legal separation, with the attendant ancillary orders, met their needs, a point taken up by the Law Reform Commission in its 1996 *Report on the Family Courts* (LRC, 1996).

In their introduction, Fahey and Lyons write of "the extraordinary level of ignorance about the social dimensions of family law" (1995: 1). More than a decade later, this statement remains true, the one shining exception being their seminal work. In the meantime the Family Law (Divorce) Act 1996 has been enacted, and the number of divorces granted in Ireland run into tens of thousands, while judicial separations continue to be sought and granted. Statutory provision exists for the adjustment of pensions after separation and divorce (see s 17 of the Family Law (Divorce) Act 1996). The regime governing the protection of victims of domestic violence has been amended (Domestic Violence Act 1996). Yet we are little wiser than we were ten years ago about the main types of family law cases other than the barest statistics: who are the clients taking them, what issues they are seeking to have addressed, and what the legal outcomes are?

This is not to say that nothing has been written on family law in Ireland since the introduction of divorce. Indeed, all the major legal publishers have published guides aimed primarily at law students and practitioners, starting with *The Law of Divorce in Ireland* by family law specialists Muriel Walls and David Bergin, published in 1997. This was followed by *The Divorce Act in Practice*, edited by Geoffrey Shannon in 1999, who followed this in 2001 with the *Family Law Practitioner*, both published by Round Hall, Sweet and Maxwell. Shannon has also written the definitive work on child law in Ireland (2005) and recently published a major review of divorce law in Ireland ten years after its enactment (2007). The same publishers also publish all the relevant pieces of family law legislation, edited by Conor Power, in the *Family Legislation Service* loose leaf, first published 2001, updated yearly. An extremely useful introduction to family law and child care law in Ireland for students and practitioners is provided by Jim Nestor (2003, 2004, 2007). All these works provide comprehensive accounts of the legislation and the case-law to date, but little by way of analysis of the law itself or comment on how it is working in practice. Essentially, they are descriptive. Books aimed at explaining family law to the general public or lay litigant include Wood and O'Shea (2003).

This does not mean that the family law system has totally escaped scrutiny. In 1996 the Law Reform Commission published a *Report on Family Courts*, which outlined many of the short-comings of the existing system and made a number of recommendations, few of which have yet to been implemented. Denham J echoed some of these recommendations, and made some fresh ones, in her *Sixth Report* of the Working Group on a Courts Commission, published in 1998.

Martin

An exception to the general dearth of critical commentary is the essay by Frank Martin, "Judicial Discretion in Family Law" (1998). Written just two years after the Family Law (Divorce) Act 1996 came into operation, it contains all too rare critical analysis of the emerging jurisprudence on divorce in Ireland, situated within the context of international debate on the issues.

He suggests that 1976, with the enactment of the Family Law (Maintenance of Spouses and Children) Act and the Family Home Protection Act, marked the end of a period of private, contract law in relation to the family in Ireland, and the dawn of a system of "flexible remedies aimed at solving particular problems in family life (that is, interventionist public law) and not always operated on a principled basis." (1998: 168)

Drawing on Dewar's criticism of family law as under-conceptualised, and weakened by the fact that "judicial decision-making is governed by vague, nebulous standards and maxims such as, for example, the 'welfare' principle", Martin states that "within Ireland, similar maxims abound" (1978: 169). Two examples are: s 20 (5) of the Family Law (Divorce) Act 1996, which refers to "in the interests of justice to do so," and in s 16(1) of the Family Law Act 1995, which speaks of a remedy "as is adequate and reasonable in the circumstances." The vagueness in the wording of the legislation is compounded by the manner in which family law is practised, according to Martin:

> "The 'rule of law' theory declares that law should be solidly reasoned, be of general application, have prospective effect, like cases should be treated alike and the law should be promulgated and announced in public. Law must also be clear, logical and above all be consistent, possessing some degree of predictability. That predictability is arrived at by a reading of the body of jurisprudence in the relevant area. Try searching the Irish law reports for a body of jurisprudence on property adjustment in marriage breakdown proceedings!" (1998: 69).

Although this was written ten years ago, not much has changed. While there is more jurisprudence on family law, this has not produced greater clarity. Indeed, as Gerry Durcan (2007: 1) has pointed out, if anything the situation is even more confusing today than it was in the immediate aftermath of the enactment of the divorce legislation.

Martin continues by criticising many of the judgments that have been published, pointing to a number of cases where no case-law is cited and no legal principles enunciated (1998: 170). He contrasts these with the judgments of McGuinness J, then a Circuit Court judge, who did cite case-law and academic texts and enunciate legal principles, as well as outlining the facts. He bemoans the fact that as a "mere" Circuit Court judge these judgments must yield to the precedent of the higher courts, a situation remedied when she became a High Court judge in 1996, and a judge of the Supreme Court in 2000, and went on to hand down a number of landmark judgments.

Martin also subjects the legislation itself to close critical analysis, pointing out that "adequacy" and "reasonableness" are "flexible, subjective and malleable concepts" (1998: 171). He points out that the *in camera* rule tends to contravene the promulgation principle (1998: 169), and examines the jurisprudence that does exist, notably on the treatment the courts should afford the "home-maker" in a situation of family breakdown (1998:174). In conclusion, he writes:

> "[I]t is highly desirable, particularly in a common law system like ours, to codify and reduce judge-made law decisions to a tolerable and flexible legal method that adheres to the rule of law maxim. Regrettably we cannot codify what does not exist" (1998: 175).

I have quoted from his paper at some length both because his arguments are compelling, and because this level of critical analysis of our family law system, both statutory and judicial, is relatively rare. In his recent book *Divorce Law and Practice*, Geoffrey Shannon, as well as outlining the recent jurisprudence, does critically examine the operation of the law on divorce and makes proposals for reform (Shannon, 2007: 338–353), but this is incidental to the main thrust of the book, which is descriptive.

Martin's criticisms are levelled at the legislation and at those judgments, normally from the higher courts, that do exist. But these now represent less than two percent of all judicial separation and divorce cases, and almost none of other areas of family law, like those involving protection and maintenance when detached from other proceedings. There the judgments are not written, and there is no stenographic record of what occurs, with only a few exceptions. One such is McMahon J, who, when he was a Circuit Court judge, did sometimes hand down written judgments in family law (see, for example, *NC v KLM,* February 22, 2002, Circuit Court, and *R v R,* January 18, 2005, Circuit Court, both unreported). There is no way of knowing whether, or to what extent, the jurisprudence being developed in the higher courts, however open to criticism it may be, is being applied in the lower courts. It is unknown, too, how precepts laid down in the legislation like "proper provision" are being interpreted and applied in these courts. Broader questions considered in other jurisdictions have not even been posed here yet.

Practitioners have also put forward certain criticisms of the existing law in practice (Walls and Bergin, 1997; Shannon, 1999 and 2007; Martin, 1998 and others). These are based on the written judgments that exist, rather than on any comprehensive knowledge of the generality of judicial decisions in family law cases. Written judgments are those that are made in the High and Supreme Court which, by definition, are usually those involving "ample resources". This means that family law jurisprudence is disproportionately focused on the issue of "proper provision" for spouses and other members of the family, rather than on other issues. The decisions of the courts on other issues, notably those concerning custody of and access to children, by and large remain a closed book.

THE *IN CAMERA* RULE
Basis for Upholding the In Camera *Rule*
A major reason for this has been the *in camera* rule in family law cases, which excluded from all family law cases not only the media, who could have informed the general public

about judicial practice in this area, but also academic researchers and interested professionals. The injunction that such cases should be heard in private may have its origins in the historical association of family life with the private world, in contrast with the public world of the state, politics and the market-place, as described by O'Donovan (1993: 23, 24). It has also been argued that relegating matters relating to the family to the private realm reinforces the domination of its stronger members over the weaker ones, that is, men over women and children (Freeman, 1985: 171, 172; Smart, 1984). Little has been written about the legal principles underlying this aspect of the law in Ireland. Shatter defends it with the brief remark, "In order to prevent unnecessary distress, it is particularly important for the protection of the parties and their family that such proceedings are held in private" without any explanation or elaboration (1997: 110).

There is little evidence that in Ireland the use of the *in camera* rule is based on upholding male power within the family. The privacy of family law proceedings has been upheld in a number of judgments (see Murphy J, *RM v DM* (Practice *in camera*) [2000] 3 IR 373), but the focus of these has been the protection of children from undue additional distress, not on the protection from public scrutiny of paternal authority. The judgment of O'Higgins CJ is representative when he said that a Sunday newspaper article about a family law case "tore away the shield of privacy which the court had erected and exposed the two children to a glare of publicity which can affect very seriously their ordinary lives, companionship at school and their relationship with their parents." (*Re McCann and Kennedy* [1976] IR 382, quoted in Shatter, 1997: 111)

Criticism of the In Camera Rule

Nonetheless, the *in camera* rule has not escaped criticism, with Mr Justice Brian Walsh writing as early as 1984:

> "The fact that most such cases are heard in camera encourages some parties to abandon all reticence and things are said and secrets are revealed which in many cases make it absolutely impossible for the parties ever to be reconciled" (preface to Binchy, 1984: viii).

Martin criticises it from the point of view of legal principle, stating:

> "*In camera* family law proceedings tend to contravene the promulgation principle. Untrained and sometimes unsympathetic judges deal indifferently with some family cases. There is an absence of a cogent and sophisticated body of legal precedents, particularly in the judicial separation ancillary orders context" (1997: 169).

In public debate, there has been much criticism of the *in camera* rule from those claiming that men's rights suffer as a result of it, which tends to undermine any argument that it is intended to benefit male power (see McCormack, 2000 and Waters, 1999–2006 for extensive criticism of the *in camera* rule, with emphasis on the man's point of view).

In 1996 the Law Reform Commission recommended that *bona fide* researchers be allowed to attend the family courts, and that information about them be made available subject to the privacy of the parties being protected (1996: 138, 139), and in 1998 the Working Group of a Courts Commission echoed many of the criticisms of this rule and recommended that it be modified (1998: 70–73). However, an attempt to implement this recommendation by the Courts Service, by appointing a barrister who would compile statistics and prepare reports of selected cases, was held, in the opinion of two separate counsels, to contravene the relevant legislation. As a result the Courts Service sought a change in the law (Report of the Family Law Monitoring Committee on the commencement, implementation and development of the Family Law Reporting Service Pilot Project, 2002, unpublished), and this finally came about in the 2004 Civil Liability and Courts Act.

L178,835

This made it possible to examine, for the first time, what is happening in the courts where the vast majority of family law takes place—the District and Circuit Courts. The Civil Liability and Courts Act became law in 2005, when those permitted to attend family law proceedings were outlined in Statutory Instrument (SI No. 337 of 2005, Civil Liability and Courts Act 2004 (s 40(3) Regulations). These included bona fide researchers attached to designated academic institutions, family mediators and those appointed by the Courts Service to prepare reports on family law. In 2006 the latter embarked on a Pilot Project on family law reporting, engaging the present author to conduct the project. This resulted in three collections of reports in the course of the pilot project, published as Family Law Matters, and a report on the project (Coulter, 2006, 2007).

While statute law is refined and defined by the superior courts in their judgments, the vast majority of people who seek the assistance of the courts in resolving their family disputes appear before the District and Circuit Courts. In 2006 98.4 percent of all judicial separations and divorces were heard in the Circuit Court, with a further 20,900 family law applications in the District Court (Courts Service, 2006: 124, 128). These courts do not create precedent in a legal sense, but their influence on the practice of the law is not to be underestimated. The decisions of the Circuit Court, in particular, are likely to influence practitioners in the advice they give their clients, and will have a significant bearing on the proportion of cases that are settled or go to full hearing.

Further, some of these decisions have made their way into the public domain through anecdote, whether or not such anecdote is accurate or representative, and therefore do contribute to a public awareness of family law, whether or not this is well-founded. The decisions of the District and Circuit Courts, therefore, form an important area of study of the practice of family law in Ireland.

Given the state of our knowledge of the workings of family law in Ireland, there is little empirical knowledge on which to base an analysis of its impact on the family and wider society. Work like that of Eekelaar, Dewar and others in the British and Australian context is a long way off. It is necessary first to establish what type of decisions are made in order to attempt to discern what patterns, if any, exist, what premises they are based on, whether these need to be challenged and whether the law needs to be changed. Broader questions, like the ideological basis of Irish family law, the extent to which it adheres to fundamental legal principles and how it relates to broader policy issues concerning the family, are yet further distant.

Absence of Debate

This almost total absence of debate about the function and impact of family legislation contrasts with the situation that pertained in the run-up to the two divorce referenda in 1986 and 1995. At that time there was much public debate about the influence of the law on individuals' behaviour and on the fabric of society, on the impact of divorce on both adults and children and about the nature of the family itself. However, with the amendment of the Constitution to permit divorce and the subsequent enactment of divorce legislation, this debate all came to an abrupt end.

This cannot be entirely attributed to the operation of the *in camera* rule. Cases involving children, whether they are the victims of abuse or sexual assault, or the subjects of adoption proceedings, or in state care, are also conducted in private. Yet the general issues at stake do make their way into the public domain, and generate considerable debate. At the moment the question of children having specific rights in the Constitution is a very live one as a result. One of the possible explanations for this is that certain judges involved in such cases have felt that they raise public interest issues and have published their judgments in a way that does not identify the children involved.

In contrast, when family law judgments from the superior courts come into the public domain the main focus of the discussion is on the division of the assets involved. There is virtually no debate on how family law legislation is being implemented, what impact this is having on families and the wider society, and whether the legislation or the manner of its implementation, or both, need reform, because the outcomes of family law in Ireland are generally unknown.

Jurisprudence on Family Law

This is largely due to the type of family law cases that make it to the higher courts. Apart from child abduction cases, the vast majority concern the division of assets. For a number of years now, the Thomson Round Hall Annual Family Law Conference has been an important arena for the updating of practitioners' knowledge of family law, and a seminal feature of that conference has been the lecture on recent case-law from Gerry Durcan SC, which he updates annually. At his lecture to the 2007 conference he described 22 cases

(Durcan, 2007: 1–100). All but one of these cases — a Circuit Court case in which the trial judge, McMahon J (as he then was, he was since elevated to the High Court) gave a written judgment concerning conduct — concerned assets worth well over €1 million, and in many cases over €10 million. With the exception of the McMahon judgment and one other, *C v C* (unreported, July 2005, High Court, O'Higgins J), where the conduct of the parties was an issue, all the cases concerned the division of the assets of the parties, and the factors to be taken into account. Only in the McMahon judgment could the resources of the couple be described as modest.

Thus the jurisprudence of family law following the introduction of divorce has been skewed towards the issue of "proper provision" in cases where there are ample resources. There is little or no jurisprudence on "proper provision" where the family's resources are limited, which is arguably a more difficult judicial task than providing for the family in "ample resource" cases. There is also very little jurisprudence concerning the welfare of children when parents separate, a matter of far greater concern to the welfare of individuals and of society than the division of assets. Issues like whether the welfare of children is best served by spending equal time with both parents, or by a regular weekly regime that might involve spending unequal amounts of time with their parents, whether it is acceptable to separate siblings when marriages break up, the use and relevance of expert testimony, whether and in what circumstances the children should be heard, what weight to give to the sex and age of the children, and a host of other matters, have received judicial consideration in the District and Circuit Courts, but these decisions are rarely written down or reported, so there is little developing jurisprudence.

Almost the only way such cases can get to the High Court and therefore generate a written judgment is by way of appeal from the Circuit Court or judicial review of an order of the District Court, unless one goes as a case stated on a point of law to the High Court. Appeals from the District Court to the Circuit Court cannot then be further appealed to the High Court, unless a judge asks for clarification on a point of law. A major obstacle to the bringing of appeals to the High Court is the question of costs. Given that the threshold for legal aid is €18,000, and the budget of the Legal Aid Board for judicial reviews is extremely limited, only the most indigent are eligible for legal aid at all, and their cases are unlikely to be judicially reviewed. The majority of other litigants either do the best they can to raise the money to pay for private legal advice, or appear as personal litigants. There are no figures for the numbers of personal litigants in the District and Circuit Courts, but Courts Service staff have estimated to this author that about half of all litigants in the Circuit Court, and more than half in the District Court, are personal litigants.

Personal litigants lack the legal knowledge to take judicial review proceedings. They are also unlikely to be able to prepare adequately an appeal to the High Court of a Circuit Court decision. Financial considerations will deter others who may be unhappy with the outcome of their cases. There is therefore a dearth of appeals from District and Circuit Court decisions, which means that these decisions have not had scrutiny either from the higher courts or from the public via the media, due to the *in camera* rule.

METHODOLOGY

The *in camera* rule has meant that there is very little empirical information about family law outcomes in Ireland, the pre-requisite for socio-legal research and for policy debate. While empirical research has its limitations, it remains the bedrock on which other types of research can build.

Dewar has remarked of socio-legal research in this area, and of outcome-driven policy reform:

> "The empirical findings of socio-legal researchers ... have been influential in the development of legal policy with respect to the family. As family law has become increasingly concerned with the consequences (or outcomes) of its rules and procedures, as opposed to the rights of the parties involved, so empirical findings have exercised a greater influence over its initial formulation, since they purport to tell us what these consequences are or might be ... [but] ... there are increasing doubts about abandoning traditional legal conceptions of rights or traditional legal methods of dispute resolution." (1992: 5)

Such a warning, from such an eminent source, should be taken seriously, but it does not undermine the argument for such empirical research in the first place, provided, of course, that the empirical information is reliable.

The use of quantitative research to attempt to describe social reality has been widely criticised, notably by the qualitative research movement and from those writing from a feminist perspective (see Agar, 1980; Silverman (ed.), 2004; Harding (ed.), 1987; Denzin and Lincoln, 2005), who argue that quantitative research does not look behind the raw data at motivation and reasons. Qualitative research would undoubtedly offer a very valuable method of ascertaining what the experience of litigants is in the family courts. However, in order to do so we would need to have a valid basis for selecting litigants to interview. This writer has adopted the approach of Seale, when he wrote, "Many practising researchers share the view, nowadays, that a variety of approaches to social research have emerged at various times ... different approaches are suited to different kinds of research problem." (2004: 6) Similarly, Miller, Dingwall and Murphy, stressing the importance of valid sources of information about outcomes and processes, said that qualitative and quantitative methods can be usefully combined (Miller *et al* in Silverman (ed.), 2004: 326), and Clough and Nutbrown offer the advice, "we adopt research stances *as they are appropriate to our work.*" (2002: 19, emphasis in the original)

As of now, we lack even enough basic information about those before the family courts to make a scientifically valid selection. The information we seek is much more basic:

1 How many people seek the resolution of their family disputes before the courts?
2 Are those initiating legal action primarily women or men?
3 How many of them settle their differences by negotiation and how many seek the court's arbitration?
4 Do these proportions vary around the country?
5 What issues are most contentious and most likely to drive people to seek the intervention of the courts?
6 What is the nature of the orders made by the courts and are these consistent?

These questions all fall within a quantitative methodology. When we have this information, it can then fall to other researchers to investigate the experience of the litigants in this process. The method I am adopting resembles that used, to great effect, by Fahey and Lyons in their pioneering work on marital breakdown in Ireland (1995).

Aim of Research

This work does not purport to answer all these questions, as such work would be beyond the resources of one individual and a limited amount of time. A comprehensive examination of all family decisions is not possible, given the volume involved. A large proportion of family law is heard in the District Court, where approximately 20,900 applications were made in 2006, the last year for which figures were available when this research was embarked upon (Courts Service Annual Report, 2006: 127–130). These concern domestic violence, maintenance and custody of and access to children, rather than the ending of marriages through judicial separation or divorce, though sometimes the Circuit Court, in deciding the latter issues, refers ancillary issues like maintenance and children to the District Court.

However, the focus of this work is on the ending of marriages through judicial separation and divorce, and the ancillary orders that are made, which is the closest the Irish legal system gets to bringing an end to a marriage. As Geoffrey Shannon has pointed out, there is no absolute clean break in Irish family law, with parties able to return to court for further ancillary orders even after the granting of a divorce decree, if circumstances radically change. (Shannon, 2007: 342). This work is concentrating, therefore, on these applications and the orders attached to them.

These applications generally go to the Circuit Court, where over 98 percent of all divorces and judicial separations were finalised in 2006 (Courts Service, 2006: 124). The majority (approximately 90 percent) of family law cases are not finally adjudicated by a judge, but are negotiated by lawyers and approved by the judge (see Ch.2 below). Initially, I intended to examine only the cases that were adjudicated by a judge in a Circuit Court, comparing whether and how ancillary orders varied from circuit to circuit, and the factors that might account for such variation. However, as I attended hearings in various circuits, it became clear that very few decisions were made following a full hearing. Often a week of family law hearings might generate no case at all that was finally decided by the judge. The week might be taken up with the judge approving settlements that had been agreed by the parties, either alone or through the efforts of their lawyers, and then made a rule of court attached to a decree of judicial separation or divorce, along with interim motions and adjournments. Sometimes cases were part-heard and then settled. Research that was limited to judicial decisions made at the end of a fully fought family law case would give a very incomplete picture of what happens in family law in Ireland, and a year's attendance at family law hearings might yield only a very unrepresentative selection of cases.

This impression was vindicated by an examination I carried out of a month's proceedings in all eight Circuit Courts, where it emerged that 91 percent of cases were settled, though sometimes after a protracted legal battle, as evidenced by the date the case was first listed and the number of appearances recorded on the file. These were then filed in court records as the granting of a decree of divorce or judicial separation, many with minimal court orders other than the extinguishing of succession orders (described as "18(10) orders" on court files, following s 18(10) of the Family Law (Divorce) Act 1996), but where the terms of the settlement were usually received and made rules of court.

I therefore decided to examine a body of outcomes, including settlements made and brought before the court, as well as attend at court proceedings. The settlements, known as "consents" would indicate the outcomes of the majority of family law cases, and would enable conclusions to be drawn about such outcomes. By comparing the outcomes in different circuits, it would also be possible to draw conclusions about variations, if there were any, between different circuits and different court venues. An examination of hearings in these circuits could further inform conclusions about the cases settled.

The methodology I adopted, therefore, was organic and dynamic, and combined empirical observation of court cases with an analysis of documentary records in the form of family files, all in the context of the legislative provisions for family breakdown and, insofar as it arose, of the relevant case-law.

It was beyond the resources of this research project to select a scientific, randomised sample of all the family law cases concluded over a year. I decided, therefore, to use a unit of time to select cases, and chose the month of October 2006 as the unit, examining all the files of all cases concluded in all eight Circuit Courts that month. This amounted to 511 cases, of which 459 were judicial separations or divorces. 1,972 judicial separations and 3,420 divorces were granted in 2006, a total of 5,392, so this represented almost 10 percent of all the judicial separations and divorces for a year, a statistically significant sample. There is no reason to think that the month of October differs significantly from other months in the type of cases dealt with.

Court Records

Not all circuits keep records in the same way. Dublin Circuit Family Court is computerised, and the orders made in cases are noted on computer records. In other circuits this is not the case, and the records are manually kept, with both outcomes and details on the paper files. While they all contain the same basic information, it is not all kept in an identical manner in all circuits. I was very grateful for the assistance of Court Service staff in accessing all the files, both electronically and manually, and making them available to me for examination.

I started this process in Dublin. Through the help of the staff in the Dublin Family Law Office it was possible to identify which cases had concluded in one month in the Dublin Circuit Court. Where the only order was the extinction of succession rights in the case of a decree of divorce, this was noted on the computer record as an 18.10 order. Where the case was disposed of with a decree of divorce or judicial separation and additional orders were made, either by consent where the agreement was made a rule of court, or on a determination of the dispute by the court, these were attached to the paper file. Armed with their case numbers, it was then usually possible to manually locate the files, which contained the written orders, both those made by the judge in the course of a judicial ruling, and those contained in the negotiated settlements known as consents. These could then be noted and analysed.

The results of this analysis are contained in Ch.2.

Circuit Court Hearings

However, it was also necessary to examine the actual process of deciding family law issues within a court-room setting, even if this often involved the formalisation of agreements already made. In addition, attendance in court provided an opportunity to talk to family law practitioners and members of the judiciary, though they were not interviewed formally and these conversations do not form part of this research project. However, they have provided insights which I was able to bring to bear on my conclusions in Ch. 4. I decided that the examination of the files and the outcomes of cases should be combined with attendance at a representative selection of family law cases. This would inform how I interpreted the written files, allow certain conclusions to be drawn about ancillary orders in contested cases, and enable me to make observations about how family law is conducted, including the extent to which reference to the legislation and to case-law determines the outcomes of family law cases.

I then proceeded to select individual Circuit Courts to attend based loosely on the volume of family law they heard. Among the Circuit Courts, the greatest volume of family law cases is, predictably, heard in the major cities. In 2005, the last year for which there were complete statistics when I began my research, Dublin heard 33 percent of all Circuit Court family law proceedings, Cork 12 percent, Limerick 5.2 percent and Galway 3.85 percent. Provincial towns on the east coast, Dundalk and Wicklow, come next, with 3.7 and 3.4 percent of all Circuit Court family law cases between them respectively. Tralee, Ennis, Naas and Clonmel heard approximately three percent each, closely followed by Wexford with 2.85 percent, Letterkenny with 2.63 percent and Waterford with 2.5 percent.

However, I considered it necessary to take factors other than mere volume into account. I felt it was essential to attend family law proceedings in all eight Circuits, six of which contain a number of counties, each having a Circuit Court in its county town. The Midland Circuit contains Laois, Longford, Offaly, Roscommon, Sligo and Westmeath, while Donegal, Cavan and Monaghan make up the Northern Circuit. No town from these counties featured as major venues for family law in 2005, yet, as towns with large rural hinterlands, which were likely to have to deal with issues relating to land, it was essential that some centres from these circuits be included. Accordingly I attended family law sittings in Birr, Portlaoise and Sligo in the Midland circuit. On the Northern Circuit Letterkenny heard 2.63 percent of all family law, while Cavan heard approximately 1.6 percent. I attended hearings in both towns.

I attended court for 76 days of the 2006/2007 legal year, starting in November. In order to form a complete picture of family law at all levels, I attended the District and High Court as well as the Circuit Court, though the major focus of my research was on the Circuit Court. If I was to relate my attendance strictly to the volume of family law cases heard by the different centres, I would have to deal in fractions of days, and would also be inhibited from hearing cases through to the end if they were adjourned. Therefore for practical reasons there is not a strict mathematical relationship between the days spent in specific courts and the volume of family law cases heard there, though there is an approximate relationship. Further, the same judge tends to hear family law cases in the different centres in each circuit, so it was of secondary importance which town was selected in each circuit. Taking into account the need to ensure that each circuit was adequately represented in the project, the need to ensure a balance between major urban centres and more rural towns, the need to follow certain cases through to their conclusion, and the problems posed by the coincidence of family law hearings in a number of different venues on the same days, the overall spread of attendance roughly corresponds to the amount of family law dealt with in that centre or in the circuit to which it belonged.

Four of the 76 days were spent in the High Court in Dublin, and 10 in Dublin District Court, including six in Court 20, which deals exclusively with child care cases. This meant I spent 62 days in Circuit Courts, and I also spent two days in Limerick with the

County Registrar attending case conferences at which cases were progressed for later hearing in the Circuit Court.

I spent 13 days in Dublin Circuit Family Court. This is less than the third merited by its proportion of all family law heard in 2005, but it made it possible to give adequate coverage to all seven other Circuits. Cork clearly was the second priority, as it deals with 12 percent of all family law, and constitutes a Circuit in itself. I spent a week there in December 2006 and again in March 2007, a total of eight days, which is approximately 12 percent of the total. Limerick is the next busiest family court, and I attended for a total of five days there in May and in July, about eight percent of the total, having spent two days with the County Registrar in case conferences in June, at which the parties and/or their solicitors met to isolate the issues in dispute, and agree what could be agreed. Two other towns on the South-Western circuit, Tralee and Ennis, each have approximately a three percent share of the Circuit Court family law. As it was not possible to visit both towns on the circuit, I attended Ennis in May for two days.

Dundalk and Wicklow are both on the Eastern circuit, and between them account for 7.5 percent of all circuit court family law cases. I visited them both for three and four days respectively, about 11 percent of the total altogether. On the Western Circuit, Galway heard 3.85 percent of all family law cases, followed by Castlebar, which hears 2.27 percent. I spent two days in each, amounting to almost seven percent of the total. On the South-Eastern Circuit, the busiest family court is Clonmel, which hears three percent, followed by Wexford with 2.85 percent and Waterford with 2.5 percent. Because of clashes with other family law hearings, I was unable to attend family law hearings in Clonmel, but I attended for a day in Nenagh, also in Co Tipperary. I spent one day in Carlow and five in Wexford, about 10 percent of the total. On the Northern Circuit, I attended family law sittings in Letterkenny for two days and Cavan for one, and on the Midland circuit I attended Sligo for three days (including returning for a case that was adjourned), Portlaoise for three and Birr for one day.

While by the end of the project I had visited all the major centres dealing with family law, it will be noted that some towns dealing with three percent or less have been omitted in favour of others with even lower volumes. This is to ensure that all Circuits have been represented in the project. I attended other towns for more than the strict percentage of family law they represented, usually because it would be artificial and impractical to break up a family law week.

My method of selecting courts did not take account of where any particular judge was sitting. Nor did I tailor my attendance to any advance notice I had of any particular case. Where I was present in court during a case where a significant issue was at stake, and where the case was adjourned, I returned to hear the rest of the case, though this could inflate the time spent in this particular court. This random, statistics-based selection of courts, though modified by other considerations, meant that some of the days' hearings I attended were devoted to very routine matters, and yielded very little either of legal interest or of interest to the general public. However, I consider that this experience reflected the reality of the totality of family law hearings.

The results of my attendance at court hearings are contained in Ch.3. These take the form both of a statistical analysis of all cases attended, and the description of a number of cases selected as representative of all those I heard. The cases are described in a manner that does not violate the anonymity of the parties, following the Protocol I developed for the reporting on family law for the Courts Service, which was approved by its Board and is still in use as the project continues.

Both Chs 2 and 3 include a significant amount of statistical analysis of outcomes of family law cases, and therefore fall more under the heading of sociological rather than strictly legal research. Where reference to case-law and to legislation is made, obviously I refer to it. The reference method I use in relation to other work is the Harvard method.

"Reactive Effect"

One issue that arose was whether my attendance affected the conduct or the outcome of the cases. This is impossible to establish, as one cannot observe without being there. The opinions of other participants, notably legal practitioners, were varied, with some suggesting that my presence influenced the conduct of the case, if not the outcome (especially if a judge was normally inclined to impatience), but in other instances my presence was not seen as a noticeable factor in the conduct of the case. Miller and Brewer have described this type of research as follows:

> "There can be advantages in overt observation because the people or groups in the setting perceive the researcher as neutral, as above members' conflicts and partisanship, and this can facilitate access to decision-making processes within the field."

Such an approach is not without its problems, however, as they also observe:

> "The gatekeeper or subjects in the field can impose constraints when the observation is overt, the researcher becomes an intervening variable in the field, influencing what is observed, and the data becomes distorted by an unknown 'reactive effect' which can restrict the ability of the researcher to get close to the people and capture life from an insider's point of view." (Miller and Brewer, 2003: 215).

This did not occur during my attendance at any court sitting. In accordance with the Rules of Court, the presiding judge drew the attention of both litigants and practitioners to my presence, and asked for any objections. They were made very rarely, and only on one occasion was I asked to leave, which I readily did, as both parties were known to me. Even then, it was a barrister for one of the parties, not the litigants, who objected, and I shared the judge's view that my attendance would be inappropriate in the circumstances.

The fact that I was already known both to members of the judiciary and legal practitioners as a journalist working in the legal area may have disposed them to accept my presence, but this is impossible to establish independently.

However, an awareness of the danger of a "reactive effect", which is undoubtedly there, cannot be allowed paralyse research, or we would never discover anything. There is no way other than by overt observation to carry out this particular piece of research, and it must suffice to warn readers that a certain element of "reactive effect" is possible in the results. Nonetheless, the normal practice in the courts is the overt observation by the public and the media of the proceedings, and they function freely within this context. The same judges are involved in public and family law proceedings, so adjusting to the conduct of family law proceedings in the presence of a researcher should not have an unduly distorting effect on their outcomes. Litigants are likely, in general, to be so preoccupied with their requirements of the process that the presence of another person in the room, whom they are assured is playing a quasi-official role, will not give rise to major concern.

Examination of Outcomes
With all these caveats, I considered it legitimate to examine family law outcomes both by examining the files of settled cases and by attending family law proceedings in order to observe how they are conducted and how judges decide on outcomes. If a dramatic difference emerged between the outcomes of cases that conclude in the presence of a researcher, and those concluded in October without any such presence, it would be appropriate to conclude that such a "reactive effect" occurred. However, no such divergence emerged.

Research in both the areas of paper files and hearings enables conclusions to be drawn on questions like the relative proportions of male and female applicants; the number of cases that are settled and the number that go to a full hearing; the factors that drive cases to a full contest; the outcomes in relation to matters like custody of and access to children, the family home, maintenance and other assets. It also enables observations to be made concerning deficiencies in the family law system, and recommendations about how it could be improved.

This research does not evaluate the litigants's own experience of the family law system. That would require qualitative research involving in-depth interviews with scientifically selected groups of litigants. Such research would undoubtedly be valuable, but it is for another researcher to carry out.

The examination of the October 2006 files, combined with attendance at courts and the interaction with members of the judiciary and practitioners, permitted me to observe how the family law system operates, and to draw some tentative conclusions as to how it could be improved for litigants. These conclusions are based on some observations of cases in the District, as well as the Circuit, Court, though only the latter are described here. While my attendance at the District Court was limited, I had the benefit of seeing reports made by members of the Courts Service Family Law Reporting Panel from these courts, which supplemented my own observations, and for which I am very grateful. These general observations, preceded by a general description of how the family law system works, are outlined in Ch.3.

In examining both the written records and the court proceedings, I looked at the profile of the litigants insofar as was possible from the information provided, which usually showed the gender of the applicant, the length of marriage and whether or not the couple had dependent children, as well as the outcomes. The outcomes were broken down according to the ancillary orders made, which normally cover the custody of and access to children, if there are any; the disposal of the family home and the provision of orders concerning maintenance and the disposal of other property. I also examined the issue of conduct if it featured as a consideration in the final orders, which are made under the legislation listed below.

The legislation covering the family law hearings I attended is the Guardianship of Infants Act 1964; the Family Law (Maintenance of Spouses and Children) Act 1976; the Family Law (Protection of Spouses and Children) Act 1981; the Domicile and Recognition of Foreign Divorces Act 1986; the Status of Children Act 1987; the Judicial Separation and Family Law Reform Act 1989; the Children Act 1989; the Family Law Act 1995; the Domestic Violence Act 1996 and the Family Law (Divorce) Act 1996 (Consolidated).

I am not concerned with a critical analysis of this legislation, but rather with an examination of how it works in practice. However, in Ch.4 I do consider how flaws in the legislation have contributed to flaws in the family law system and put forward some tentative suggestions for changes.

Chapter 2

OUTCOMES AS RECORDED IN COURTS SERVICE FILES FOR OCTOBER 2006

Discussion on how Irish family law is functioning has been severely hampered by the lack of information. Not only have the courts been closed to observers because of the *in camera* rule (modified by the Civil Liability and Courts Act 2004, as described in Ch.1), statistics on what happens in court, shorn of all identifying details, have also been limited. The Courts Service has published global statistics on the numbers of divorces, judicial separations, nullity, maintenance and domestic violence orders applied for and granted each year, but it has not, so far, been possible to break down these figures further (see Courts Service Annual Report 2006: 123–131).

Doing so is a task for statisticians and IT professionals, but some knowledge of how the family courts are working will be available from a study of a sample of court records, which contain case outcomes and orders made. Where cases are concluded by consent, the terms of the consent are normally made a rule of court and filed in the court records. Where the judge makes the ruling, his or her decisions are recorded as orders of the court.

In 2005, the last year for which figures were available at the outset of this research, 99 percent of all divorces and judicial separations were granted by the Circuit Court. In 2006 the figure was 98.4 percent (Courts Service Annual Report 2006: 124). This is probably due to the extended jurisdiction of the Circuit Court, which now can, and does, hear family law cases worth up to €10 million. This therefore forms the most important arena for examination of the development of family law in the State since the introduction of divorce.

Court records are kept in different ways in different circuits, with the orders made recorded on computer records in Dublin, supplemented by consents made rules of court and attached to paper files. In other circuits all the information is contained in the paper files. With the assistance of Courts Service staff I identified the files relating to the cases in which orders were given during the month of October 2006, and then examined the files, noting the information contained in them in relation to the applicants and to the orders made, and information taken from any consents that were appended to the files.

I am not a statistician, and the files are not kept with the objective of recording information for statisticians or social scientists, but rather with a view to recording orders and enabling the court to ensure they were complied with. Therefore the type of information kept in the files was not uniform across all the circuits, nor is the same amount of information retained on the files in all of them. Thus, the data collected was not uniform throughout the circuits. Further, the gender of applicants was not always clear from the files, so the total numbers under the gender headings do not add up to the total number of cases. Nonetheless, the information outlined below represents common denominators found in the files of all eight circuits. As I was seeking to identify issues that were either in dispute or solved, many cases contained two or more such issues, so some cases are counted more than once in the totals given below. I have checked all the figures several times, and am confident the figures detailed below are accurate to within one or two percent.

As stated above, I decided to choose a "snapshot" rather than a sample of cases, taking the month of October 2006 as the period of time from which I would examine the files on all cases concluded that month. They came to 511, of which 459 were judicial separations and divorces. This was almost 10 percent of all family law decided in the Circuit Court in 2006, a considerably greater proportion than the sample taken by polling organisations in conducting professional surveys.

In all but three circuits the cases that were concluded following a full hearing and a judicial ruling were so few as to not permit a meaningful comparison with the cases that were settled and had the terms made a rule of court. However, contested and settled cases are compared in the three circuits where this was justified by the numbers, and they are compared at the end of this chapter where all the statistics are combined in order to examine national trends.

Dublin Circuit Court

I examined the cases listed on the Courts Service computer system for the Dublin Circuit Family Court which were initiated back to the beginning of 2003, the first year in which all cases were logged on the new computerised system, and identified cases decided between October 3 and 31, 2006. I identified 183 cases decided that month, including 22 appeals from the District Court, leaving 161. From the computer records I was able to see how long they took, how many were settled, how many went to a full hearing, and what orders were made. Orders for judicial separation and divorce also usually gave the date of the marriage, so it was possible to see the variation in the duration of the marriages that ended in separation or divorce.

Type of Application

Most of the cases concerned judicial separation and divorce, with eight falling under the heading of "other". In the majority of these cases it was possible to discern the gender of the applicant by first name (though in some instances this was ambiguous, and these cases were left out of the calculation). Gender could be deduced definitively in 141 cases, of which 44 were judicial separations and 97 were divorces. Women outnumbered men dramatically in seeking judicial separation, by 38 to six, but men outnumbered women in seeking divorce, where there were 53 male applicants and 44 female. Overall, there were 82 female applicants and 59 male.

The bulk of cases decided in October 2006 had been initiated earlier that year, with 99 out of the total of 161 initiated in the first nine months of 2006, indicating that cases did not necessarily take long to get to trial or settlement, if both parties were willing to reach a conclusion. The fastest case recorded for that month took only four days. It concerned a divorce where the papers were lodged on October 23 and the order granted on October 27. According to court staff, an order can be rushed through in cases where one of the parties is terminally ill. Apart from that, the shortest case took six weeks from initial application to final order.

Of the 99 cases originating in 2006, 83 were divorce applications where both parties consented to the terms of the divorce. In over 60 of these cases the only order made was a blocking order, extinguishing the inheritance rights of both parties against the estate of the other. In a further 11 cases a blocking order was accompanied by a Pension Adjustment Order, most of which were nominal rather than substantial. Therefore in only nine of the divorce cases decided on consent were other issues, like the family home, other property, maintenance and the custody of children part of the settlement, and filed as a rule of the court.

This suggests that many of these issues are decided earlier in the process, when the divorce applicants have negotiated a separation agreement or gone through a judicial separation. By the time they fulfil the condition of having lived separate and apart for four of the past five years, most of them will have resolved the most contentious issues and moved on in their lives.

Ten of the 12 applications for judicial separation that were initiated that year ended in consents, with the terms filed as schedules or rules of court. Of the remaining 2006 cases, three (one divorce and two judicial separations) went to full hearings and judgment, and four concerned other matters like guardianship.

There were fewer divorces by consent among the cases initiated in earlier years. Fourteen of the divorces granted in October on consent had been initiated in 2005, one in 2004, and six in 2003. Of the judicial separations granted, 13 of those begun in 2005 ended in consent terms, nine of those initiated in 2004, and five of those begun in 2003. Of all the 161 cases concluded in October, 103 of the divorces and 33 of the judicial separations ended in settlement. This left nine divorces and seven judicial separations that went to a full hearing, ending in a judicial decision. Nine of the cases concerned other matters like guardianship and declarations of parentage.

These figures showed that the longer the proceedings go on, the less likely the parties are to agree to a consent order, though some still do. They also show that in Dublin that month only about 10 percent of family law cases were contested to the end. Contrary to popular perception, the majority of family law cases are settled, and the people concerned get on with their lives.

It is clear from the files, however, that the settlement can come at various stages in the process, and may follow years of bitter dispute and protracted negotiations. Cases begun in 2003 or 2004, for example, had often gone through a number of hearings on matters like discovery and access to children before ending up with a settlement. Sometimes such settlements are accompanied by court orders, like pension and property adjustment orders. As will be shown when court hearings are examined, it is likely that many of these hearings could be avoided (see Ch.3). It appeared from the files on some cases, where anything up to 20 court appearances can be registered, that a long battle preceded the final settlement. I will examine the policy implications of this finding in Ch.4.

Other cases have ended with a high level of agreement between the former spouses. The number of divorces where the only orders made were blocking orders, extinguishing each other's succession rights, is indicative of that, suggesting a clear preference on the part of many couples for a "clean break" end to their marriages. However, as Geoffrey Shannon has pointed out, under the Irish Constitution and law spouses may return to court at any time to review the arrangements made under the "proper provision". (Shannon, 2007: 341, 342)

Contested Cases

At the other end of the spectrum lie the cases that were contested all the way. Here the most contentious issues would appear to relate to custody of children and maintenance. Eleven of the 16 fully contested cases involved children. In six of them joint custody was ordered, usually with the child or children living with the mother and access either as agreed between the parties or as laid down by the court following hearing of the evidence. Court-ordered access can include complex arrangements to ensure that the child spends substantial amounts of time with both parents.

In three of the cases the mother was granted sole custody, and in one of these the father did not appear in court, while in another he was granted only supervised access to the children, suggesting allegations of abuse found credible by the court. In two of the cases no orders about custody were made, though there were orders concerning maintenance.

Maintenance

Maintenance was an issue in 11 cases. The amounts of maintenance ordered varied widely, presumably reflecting the different circumstances of the applicants. In one case a maintenance payment of €8 a week per child was ordered, while at the other end of the spectrum a husband was ordered to pay €1,550 a month, of which €650 was for the wife and €300 for each of the three children. This was the only case where maintenance for both the wife and children was ordered on an ongoing basis, until the children reached the age of 18, or 23, if in full-time education. In a case where substantial property was divided the husband was ordered to pay €866.66 a month for the maintenance of the couple's child. In one case, the only maintenance was a contribution from the husband of €300 at Christmas. There is no way, from the Court Service records, of knowing what the income of the husband was in either case.

In general, however, the maintenance payments ordered by Dublin Circuit Court in October were in the region of €100 to €150 a week per child. In two cases maintenance had already been set by the District Court, and the amounts were not recorded. There was one case where there were no dependent children and maintenance, of €120 a week, was ordered for the wife.

Family Home
The fate of the family home was also decided upon in 11 of the 16 contested cases. It was ordered to be sold in five cases, with the proceeds divided either 50/50 (three cases) or 60/40 (larger share to the husband in one case, to the wife in the other). In two of the cases the house was to be sold when the youngest child was no longer dependent, and the proceeds then divided 50/50. In many of these cases two or more issues were decided at the same time. In two cases the husband's interest was transferred to the wife, and in two she had the right to occupy the family home for life. In both these latter cases the maintenance ordered for the children was negligible (€8 per child per week in one, none in the other), suggesting the transfer of the husband's interest was in lieu of maintenance, though this was not stated. In one of the remaining cases where the family home was transferred to the wife there was no appearance on behalf of the husband, and in the other a divorce was granted with no other orders.

In two cases pension adjustment orders were adjourned, and in one the husband's retirement lump sum and the family's savings were ordered to be split 50/50. There was also a case where three additional properties were ordered to be sold along with the family home, and the proceeds divided 50/50 between the husband and wife.

Duration of Marriage
The length of a marriage does not seem to be a major factor in whether it ends in divorce or judicial separation though it may affect the orders made. Among the divorces granted, three were to people who had been married more than 40 years, and 18 were granted to people married more than 30 years. The rest were sprinkled fairly evenly among those married for periods ranging between six and 30 years.

The date of the granting of a divorce does not, of course, necessarily indicate when the marriage ended. Divorces are often sought years after a separation, either by separation agreement or judicial separation, where the affairs of the two parties are effectively separated and matters concerning children, maintenance and property sorted out. The number of divorces granted where the only orders sought were those extinguishing succession rights suggests that such earlier agreements were already in place.

The duration of a marriage before a judicial separation is sought may be a better indicator of when marriage breakdown occurs. However, here too there is a wide spread, with two couples obtaining a judicial separation after less than five years of marriage, and one doing so after 40 years. Three judicial separations were granted to people after more than 30 years of marriage.

Consents

Sixty-four of the cases concluded in the Dublin Circuit Family Court in October had consents filed in court. Forty-eight of these consents were available for analysis of the terms, 28 linked to judicial separation, 18 to divorce, and two to guardianship. In the cases where no consents were filed, this usually meant a divorce was agreed with mutual blocking orders (extinguishing succession rights) only.

Agreements relating to children were made in 21 of these cases, with custody and access referred to in 18 of them. In 16 of the cases joint custody was agreed, with the child or children residing primarily with the mother in 11 of them, and sharing time equally in five. In two the wife had sole custody, with access for the husband. In most cases access was either "as agreed", or according to detailed arrangements handed in to the court, normally specifying that the child or children would spend two weekends a month and at least one week night with the father, with further detailed arrangements for festival periods and holidays. In one case the wishes of the children were mentioned in relation to access.

In most, but not all cases, the father agreed to pay maintenance for the children. The amounts varied from €100 per child per month to €173 a week (€700 a month approx). In two of the cases no maintenance was agreed, apart from VHI cover in one, and in the other the wife acknowledged that the husband was getting less than his fair share of the family home in lieu of maintenance. In two other cases no maintenance was agreed apart from half the child or children's educational and medical expenses. In the 13 other cases where monetary amounts were agreed, the average rate was just over €400 a month. Only in three cases was the amount agreed less than €75 a week.

It was relatively rare for wives to be paid maintenance, and the amounts varied widely. In two cases where dependent children were also being paid maintenance, the wives were paid €400 and €580 a month. In one of the three cases where maintenance was being paid to the wives where there were no dependent children, €571.38 a month was being paid for four months until she became eligible for the non-contributory old age pension, when this would cease. However, in this case she did receive ownership of the family home. In one of the other cases where the wife received maintenance for herself alone, the amount was €400 a month, while in the other it was almost four times that.

It is clear from the consents that couples prefer a "clean break" to the ongoing link represented by maintenance, despite the fact that the law does not allow for total finality. This seems to be often achieved by apportioning the family home disproportionately, in lieu of maintenance. There were also a few lump sums paid.

The family home was dealt with in 43 of the 46 cases. In 26 of these the family home was transferred to the wife, normally on payment by her of a sum varying between €20,000 and €320,000. Explanations for these sums are not recorded, but that could vary from the value of the house and the amount left to be paid on the mortgage, to whether or not maintenance was being paid as well. It was often, but not always, specified that the wife would take over paying the mortgage, and in one case the husband continued to pay the mortgage. In four of the cases either the wife already had ownership of the house, or she was permitted to live in it without ownership being specified, and in three of the cases it was agreed that it be transferred to the husband, for the sums of €10,000, €110,000 and €210,000 respectively.

In the 10 remaining cases it was agreed that the family home be sold, and the proceeds divided. The ratio of the division ranged from 50/50 (in three instances) to 75/25, with the average range being 45 percent to the husband and 55 percent to the wife.

Pensions and other assets were dealt with in 42 of the cases dealt with, but in the majority of these pensions were referred to only to specify that no claim was being made on the pension of either party, or a nominal Pension Adjustment Order was being made (typically for 0.001 percent of the pension based on one day's earnings). In two of the cases it was agreed that the wife should receive 50 percent of the husband's pension, and in two others that she remain the beneficiary of his contingent pension (in the event of death). In another the wife was to receive a refund of his pension contributions.

The most common form of other financial adjustment was provision for the payment of life assurance, either to guarantee maintenance of children or the payment of a mortgage. Such payments were agreed in six cases. In another case the wife received half the family's savings, and in the one case where significant resources appeared to exist, a property in addition to the family home was transferred to the wife, along with €25,000 towards her legal costs. In this case, which involved a divorce after 36 years of marriage, a High Court maintenance order was discharged, so there was a transfer of property but no ongoing financial support. In 20 of the 42 cases, the parties specifically stated that they had no claim on each other's pension or other assets.

In 13 of the 28 judicial separation consents one of the clauses was that the consent constituted "full and final" settlement, or that it was binding in future divorce proceedings. In fact, such an undertaking cannot bind the court, though it can have regard to it in future applications for ancillary relief. In two of the divorce consents it was also stated that this was a "full and final" settlement. However, as case-law has shown, these may not be found to be binding, and they are not provided for in the legislation, other than that the court can have regard to them (s 14 Family Law (Divorce) Act 1996). While Hardiman J indicated that such a clause could bring finality in *WA v MA (WA v MA* [2005] 1 IR 1), Finlay-Geoghegan J came to a different conclusion in *RG v CG (RG v CG* [2005] IR 418), and in *JC v MC* Mr Justice Abbott devoted considerable attention to the issue, distinguishing between the affect such clauses might have on lump sums and on ongoing maintenance (High Court delivered in October 2007, unreported).

CORK CIRCUIT COURT

The second busiest Circuit Court dealing with family law is Cork Circuit Court, which in 2005 heard 10 percent of all divorces, judicial separations, nullity applications and District Court appeals. Two weeks were devoted to family law in Cork in October 2006, and only one court sat, presided over by O'Donohue J, compared with two full-time and one part-time family law courts sitting in Dublin the same month. Fifty cases were disposed of in these two weeks. Two were judicial separations that were abandoned with divorce applications substituted, as the requisite four years' separation requirement had been met. These were then adjourned. Of the remaining 48, 40 were divorces and eight were judicial separations. No District Court appeals, guardianship applications, nullities, declarations of parentage or similar matters were decided that month.

Women significantly outnumbered men in seeking divorces, with 24 female applicants and 16 males. In applying for judicial separations the figures were inverted, with five husbands making applications, compared with three women, though the figures here are too small to allow conclusions to be drawn. Overall, there were 27 female applicants and 21 male.

All the cases were settled, though this does not mean the settlement was always amicable. Some of the terms indicate considerable discord before the settlement, with the file recording several appearances, and, in some instances, motions for discovery.

The majority of the cases (33) were initiated in 2006, with 13 applications having been made in 2005. Two of the cases went back to 2004. As was the case in Dublin, there was no single age-group dominant among those who ended their marriage in judicial separation or divorce. The length of marriage ranged from less than five years (one judicial separation) to over 30 years, the largest single group (11) being couples married between 21 and 25 years.

Judicial Separations

Children

Six of the eight judicial separations agreed concerned dependent children. In five cases joint custody was agreed, with the primary residence with the mother. In the sixth case the child was 18 and in full-time education, living with the mother, and no custody or access was mentioned. There were no children in two cases. In all instances where access was mentioned it was stated to be agreed, with specific times mentioned. In no case was there any indication that either party had initially sought a different outcome.

Maintenance

Maintenance ranged from €1,000 a month for two children to €65 a week for the student, to be reduced if he worked in the summer. In three other cases where there were two children in each case the maintenance was €125 a week, €190 a week and €200 a week respectively. There was no spousal maintenance paid in any case.

Family Home

The family home was transferred to the wife on payment of a sum in three cases, and to the husband, also on payment of a sum, in two. In one case no transfer was agreed, but the children were to live in the family home with the mother. In the two remaining cases no reference was made to the family home. There were two nominal pension adjustment orders agreed, and one transfer of pension entitlement. The making of "nominal" pension adjustment orders, where one day's contribution is taken as the basis of the order, rendering it meaningless, appears to be favoured by some solicitors in order to prevent the issue of the pension arising later.

A noticeable feature of the judicial separation decrees made on consent was that six of the eight contained a "full and final" settlement clause, stating that the financial arrangements come to were intended by the parties to be final.

Divorces

It was striking in relation to the divorce cases that the majority were settled with very few additional orders, indicating that the settlement was amicable. In half the 40 divorces granted on consent a previous legal or judicial separation was in place, and the terms of the separation were imported into the divorce settlement and made a rule of court. Eighteen such judicial separation consents were included in the divorce files, and in two cases they were referred to, but not included in the file.

In seven of the remaining divorce cases the only orders made in addition to the decree of divorce was an order mutually extinguishing the parties' succession rights (known as an 18(10) order). In some of these there may have been separation terms in place, but these were not referred to or made rules of court. It is equally possible that these divorces followed long years of separation when the parties had established independent lives and wanted to bring a formal end to their marriages.

In the remaining 13 cases, where there had not been a separation agreement in place, the issues settled ranged from the disposal of the family home, to other property issues, to children. In two of the cases the house was sold and the proceeds divided 50/50 between the spouses, in one it was transferred into two names, and there were three instances of the husband and the wife buying out the other spouse. In four cases there were other financial orders, including one where a considerable amount of property was divided.

Custody

The figures for all the circuits show that children are the most contentious issue in family law proceedings. It is likely that the most contentious issues are dealt with when the couple seeks a judicial separation, which under s 2 (1)(d) and s 2 (1)(f) of the Judicial Separation and Family Law Reform Act 1989, can be done a year after the breakdown of the marriage. When a divorce is sought, the Constitution (Art 41.3) and s 5 of the Family Law (Divorce) Act 1996 require that the couple be separated for a minimum of four years, and issues relating to the children may have been largely resolved by this stage, or the couples may be older, with children no longer dependent.

In the 19 divorce cases where the question of children was dealt with, joint custody was agreed in 11. In eight of these the child's primary residence was with the mother, and in two of them this issue was referred to the District Court, while in one this was left to the wishes of the child. In four of the remaining eight the child's residence and/or access was shared equally between the parents, or some children lived with each parent. In two cases custody went to the mother alone, and in two to the father alone. These trends are to be seen elsewhere, and I will attempt to draw some conclusions about them at the end of this chapter.

The background to sole, rather than joint, custody was not indicated in the files, but, based on cases I have attended, it often reflects a lack of involvement on the part of the other parent in the child's life prior to the divorce.

Maintenance

Maintenance was generally paid for children, but only rarely for a dependent spouse. In 17 cases the payment of maintenance was agreed, including three cases where some spousal maintenance was agreed. Inevitably, the amounts varied depending on the means of the family, but generally it fell in the range of €400–€500 a month per child. However, in some instances it was as little as €20. There were no instances of a mother paying maintenance to the father. Small levels of maintenance could reflect the fact that some settlements involved the children spending a considerable proportion of their time with the father, who was therefore bearing the cost of their upkeep.

Financial Orders

There were nine other financial orders made, normally involving a lump sum. While 16 pension adjustment orders were made, nine of them were only nominal. The family home was disposed of in 25 cases, with it being sold and the proceeds divided in four of them. In 15 cases the wife bought out the husband's interest in the house, and in six the husband bought out the wife's interest. In the remainder of cases the couple lived in rented accommodation, they already had their own houses, or there was no reference to a family home.

SOUTH-WESTERN CIRCUIT COURTS

The third largest centre in the state for family law is Limerick, having processed five percent of all judicial separations and divorces in 2006. The counties of Limerick, Kerry and Clare make up the South-Western Circuit, therefore I am taking them together for the purposing of analysing case outcomes in October 2006.

The South-Western Circuit is the only Circuit to contain both a large city (Limerick), serving a mainly urban population, and two smaller county towns (Ennis and Tralee) serving substantially rural and small town populations. It is therefore the only Circuit able to show differences between a mainly urban and mainly rural and small town population base by contrasting the outcomes in the different Circuit Courts within it.

Statistics also show Limerick has a higher concentration of family problems than other cities and towns. For example, it has the highest number of separated people (13 percent) while Galway has the lowest (six percent). (O'Brien, *Irish Times*, October 31, 2008). It also has the highest number of births outside marriage, with the CSO 2006 annual summary revealing that 57.2 percent of all births in Limerick were non-marital, compared with 32.2 percent national average (Treoir, August 2007; 3)

It must be remembered that the city boundaries do not contain much of the city's suburbs, which will inevitably have a distorting effect on such statistics. Family law litigants in Limerick Circuit Court will include residents of the city, its suburbs and from the county itself, but residents of the city itself are likely to make up a significant proportion of all litigants.

Limerick Circuit Court was the third-busiest in the State for family law in 2005, after Cork and Dublin.

Due to pressure of business, Limerick began the Michaelmas term early in 2006, with a week of family law at the end of September. I took this as the equivalent of October hearings in other circuits. In October there was also a week of family law in Tralee, but none in Ennis. Tralee and Limerick therefore heard all the South-Western Circuit's family law that month.

Differences between Tralee and Limerick

In order to retain consistency across all the circuits I am amalgamating the figures so that a total is shown for the whole circuit. However, significant differences can be seen between the two counties in a number of areas, probably due to the more urban nature of family law in Limerick, and I outline these below. This contrast was particularly obvious in this circuit, for reasons referred to above.

The most glaring difference was to be seen in settlement rates. There were significantly more contested cases in Tralee than in Limerick, with nine of the total number of 32 cases fought to the end, culminating in a judicial decision, a settlement figure of only about 73 percent. Six of the fought cases were divorce, and three judicial separations. In contrast, only two of the 48 cases heard in Limerick were fully contested, of which one was a divorce and one a judicial separation, giving a settlement rate of 96 percent. Uniting the two centres, 11 of the 80 cases were fully contested, with a settlement rate of about 88 percent, slightly below the average for Dublin for the same month, and in contrast with Cork in that period, when all were settled.

A contributory factor to the more contentious nature of cases in Tralee may be that there was a much higher proportion of judicial seperations and a higher proportion included decisions involving dependent children. There were 17 cases involving children in Tralee, out of a total of 32, that is, over half of all the cases, but only 13 in Limerick, out of a total of 48, just over a quarter. It may be that contentious cases were grouped together for hearing in that particular family law session in Tralee.

It may also be relevant that in Limerick 19 of the cases involved marriages more than 25 years old, while in Tralee only nine cases involved couples married more than 25 years. The children of couples in the older age-range are unlikely to be still dependent, so their future and welfare will not be an issue in a judicial separation or a divorce. On the other hand, there is likely to be a higher level of dependency among spouses in the older age-group, which could be reflected either in maintenance being paid to the dependent spouse, or in the allocation of proportions of the family home.

There was a difference also between the two centres in relation to the family home and other assets. In Limerick the family home was not an issue in 16 of the cases. In four cases this was because each party already has a house, usually because a divorce followed a judicial separation which laid the basis for each of them establishing an independent life. However, in 12 cases the family home was not an issue because one or both of the parties lived in rented accommodation, or with relatives. In Tralee both parties already had houses in six cases, and neither had one in seven.

In the two weeks' family law in the South-Western Circuit a total of 80 cases were disposed of, 48 in Limerick and 32 in Tralee. This compared with 50 cases in Cork in two weeks in the same month. Eight were judicial separations in Tralee, and two in Limerick. Thus 25 percent of the Tralee cases were judicial seperations, while only 5 percent of the Limerick ones were. There were 24 divorces in Tralee and 44 in Limerick. Limerick also heard one recognition of an English divorce and one declaration of parentage, both on consent. There were no District Court appeals, guardianship applications or nullities.

Duration of Marriage

As has been seen in Dublin and Cork, there was a wide spread of age-group among those seeking judicial separation and divorce. While dates of birth are not on the files, the dates of the marriages are, showing the length of the marriage and providing a rough indication of the ages of the parties.

Five of the 32 applications in Tralee and 11 of the 48 in Limerick came from couples married less than 10 years; 11 in each centre came from couples married between 11 and 20 years; ten in Tralee and 12 in Limerick were from couples married between 21 and 30 years, while six marriages in Tralee and 13 in Limerick ended formally after more than 30 years. It was clear from the orders than in the some of the cases, but not in most, this happened after many years of separations. In a significant number of divorce cases a judicial separation or a separation agreement was already in place, and the divorce merely finalised the end of the marriage.

Gender

Women outnumbered men by 48 to 32 in seeking an end to their marriages through separation or divorce. However, this happened more frequently with judicial separation, where of the 10 judicial separations sought, eight were by woman. While women outnumbered men in seeking divorces, (by 39 to 31) the contrast was not so marked.

Custody

Children emerged again as a contentious issue, with five of the nine cases that went to a full hearing in Tralee involving children. There were 17 child-related cases in Tralee in all, so 12 of those in Tralee were settled by agreement. There were 15 child-related cases in Limerick, of which two were contested. Thus there were 32 child-related cases in all, of which seven were contested.

The outcome of the contested cases did not differ significantly from that of those that were settled. In terms of custody, normally the most contentious issue, three of the contested cases ended in sole custody being granted to the mother, and joint custody being granted in the other four. Among that four, in one the child or children's primary residence was with the mother, in one some children were with each parent, in one they had shared residency between the two homes, and in one the matter was referred to the District Court.

Some examples illustrate the background to such cases. In one the eight-year-old child had been visited by its father only once since the marriage broke up six years earlier. The court granted sole custody to the mother, with access to be agreed. There were no family home and no financial orders. In another case an order for joint custody was made during a divorce application, setting aside a 2001 District Court order granting sole custody to the mother. During another divorce application, where the mother claimed the husband had deserted the family 13 years earlier and had no relationship with the children, sole custody was granted to her.

Among the settled cases, the mother was granted sole custody in eight. Joint custody was ordered in 17 cases, with the primary residence with the mother in eight, with the father in one, shared between the parents in three and some children living with each parent in two. No primary residence was specified in three cases, usually indicating that the children are older and decide themselves where they live, or are in full-time-third level education.

There was some difference in outcome between the cases in Tralee and those in Limerick. Joint custody, with either no primary residence specified or with primary residence with the mother, was by far the most likely outcome in Tralee (12 out of the 17 cases), while in Limerick, in eight out of the 15 cases the mother was granted sole custody, with joint custody granted in just six cases, three of them specifying that the primary residence was with the mother. Sole custody to the mother was the outcome in only four out of the 17 cases in Tralee.

In one case in Tralee joint custody was accompanied by the child living primarily with the father. In two cases it was specified that the father was not to have custody in any circumstances, including the death of the mother. Access was generally "as agreed", though this did not necessarily mean it had been agreed in advance. In a number of cases the father did not appear in court, and, while access was to be agreed, disputes about it were to go to the District Court. Access was shared jointly in four of the Tralee cases and in three of the Limerick cases.

Maintenance

Maintenance of the children arose less than may have been expected, with no maintenance orders made in nine of the Tralee cases and four of the Limerick cases. Where maintenance was agreed or ordered, the amounts ranged from under €30 a week per child (three cases) to between €50 and €100 (eight cases). There was no discernable difference in the amount of maintenance ordered in the contested cases or agreed in the settled cases. In two cases the amount agreed was between €30 and €50 per child. It was referred to the District Court in two cases, and in another two a lump sum was paid in lieu. Maintenance of spouses was relatively rare (only agreed or granted in five of the 80 cases).

Family Home

In most divorces and judicial separations the main asset is the family home. Various solutions emerge in its disposition, probably (though this is not clear from the paper files) linked to whether or not there are dependent children. These solutions can include one party buying out the other's interest; the family home being transferred to one or other party without payment, but usually with this party taking over the payment of the mortgage; or the sale of the family home and the distribution of the proceeds. In some divorce cases the family home has already been disposed of in a legal separation or in judicial separation proceedings, and the parties now each have their own homes.

There is also a group of people who do not own a family home, and normally have lived as a couple in local authority or private rented accommodation. Occasionally a couple may have lived with relatives, usually in-laws. Sometimes another family member may have contributed to the acquisition of the family home, and their interest is recognised when it comes to be disposed of.

In a small minority of cases there are substantial assets to be distributed, of which the family home is only one. In such cases it is common for one party to get the family home without compensating the other party for his or her interest, while the other party gets other family assets, for example, land, a public house, rental properties or other investments.

In seven of the Tralee cases and six of the Limerick cases the family home was transferred to the wife without her paying for her husband's interest, but usually with her taking on the mortgage. In four of the Tralee cases and five of the Limerick ones the house was transferred to the wife by her buying out her husband's interest; in one Tralee case and four Limerick cases the opposite occurred.

The house was sold and the proceeds divided (usually, but not always, 50/50) in two of the Tralee and five of the Limerick cases. In six Tralee cases each party had his or her own house, while this was the case in only four of the Limerick cases. In contrast, there was no family home at issue in 12 of the Limerick cases because neither party owned a house, while this was the case in only seven of the Tralee cases. The house was left in joint names in one case in Tralee and three in Limerick, with one party having the right to reside in it for a specified period of time and the parties' respective shares allocated when it would come to be sold.

Other financial assets were divided in three Tralee and six Limerick cases. Pensions did not emerge as a major issue in either centre, with no significant allocation of a pension in Tralee and only one in Limerick. Nominal pension adjustment orders were made in a handful of cases.

It was not entirely clear from the files why some cases went to a full hearing and a judicial decision. Of the 11 where that happened, four were judicial separation and seven divorce applications. The family home and children appeared to be the most contentious issues. In one case where the only orders made concerned the family home the husband was allocated €60,000 of its value by the Circuit Court. He appealed to the High Court, where he was given €65,000. It is likely the costs of the application exceeded the difference.

The family home featured in 10 of the 11 cases that were contested. In two cases it was ordered to be sold and the proceeds divided; in four it was transferred to the wife's name, normally by her paying the husband a sum and/or taking over the mortgage; in one it had already been disposed of; in one case it was to be sold later when the children were grown up; and in two cases the interest in it held by each party was declared.

In one such contested case the court ordered the transfer of the family home to the wife's sole name, without any payment. It also made an order extinguishing the husband's succession rights, but not the wife's. An order that the children live with the mother was not contested. A second case also saw the court extinguish the succession rights of the husband, but not the wife. No other orders were made. The background to neither of these cases was given, but there may have been a history of abandonment with no maintenance paid for a number of years, and the maintenance of the wife's succession rights may have been an attempt to compensate for this, as this was the attitude the court took to such circumstances in cases I observed, as outlined in Ch. 3.

The only order (other than the usual orders granting a decree and extinguishing succession rights) in another case was for the sale of the family home, with the husband's interest set at 15 percent. In a further case there was a readjustment of the interest in the family home, where an earlier judicial separation had granted 60 percent to the wife and 40 percent to the husband. When it came to a divorce the husband sought to buy out his wife's interest, the value of which was now set at €93,000. Existing arrangements concerning the two children, where one lived with each parent, continued.

In a divorce case where the family home was owned by a local authority, the court declared that the husband, who had been the subject of barring and protection orders over a 20-year period, had no interest in it. No other orders were made. In a judicial separation case involving an Irish woman and a non-Irish-national man, where the marriage had been short and there were no children, succession rights were extinguished and the court made an order that no mutual eligibility existed under the Family Home Protection Act 1976.

Among the settled cases, the family home was sold and the proceeds divided in five cases, and transferred into the wife's name in 16. It was transferred into the husband's name in five, and the husband was given the right to reside in it in one. Both parties had houses in three cases, and the house was already disposed of in eight. Declarations of interest were made in two, and neither spouse had a home, or none was referred to, in the remaining 29.

The picture that emerges from the total number of cases decided in the South-Western Circuit, however, is that the great majority of judicial separations and divorces are finalised here, as in Cork and Dublin, by an agreement between the parties, though this is sometimes after a number of court appearances and even after the hearing of some evidence.

EASTERN CIRCUIT COURTS

The Eastern Circuit is one of the busiest outside Dublin, and over 70 cases were finalised there in October 2006. The Eastern Circuit includes the counties of Louth, Meath, Wicklow and Kildare, all of which have greatly expanded their population in recent years and contain a large commuter population. This is reflected in the volume of family law passing through the courts. There were two family law sittings in the Eastern Circuit in October 2006, in Wicklow and Naas, and between them they finalised 71 cases.

In four of these cases the files were incomplete, and so have been omitted from the analysis. Two more were appeals from the District Court, one concerning a successful appeal on application for guardianship of an infant, and the other an appeal on access that was settled on the day of the appeal. This left 65 cases, 17 judicial separations and 48 divorces, of which two were fully contested in court. One of these cases involved children, the other purely financial matters. This gave a settlement rate of over 95 percent, though it is clear from the files that some of the settlements came at the very last minute, on the eve of the planned court hearing.

Gender

Of the 17 judicial separations, 13 were initiated by women and four by men. Among the divorces, 30 were initiated by women and 18 by men. Overall, therefore, 43 of the applications were made by women and 22 by men.

Deeds of separation or judicial separations existed in only seven of the divorce cases, less than in other circuits on the same month. Given that a couple must have lived apart for four out of the five preceding years before seeking a divorce, this might indicate that a higher proportion of people were content with informal separation arrangements before making a divorce application.

Custody

In 32 of the cases there were no dependent children, including both cases of couples who had never had children (the minority) on the one hand, and those whose children had grown up on the other. In a few cases there was no reference on the file to children at all. In 19 of the 29 cases where children were referred to in the court documents the outcome was joint custody between the parents with primary care and control resting with the mother. In all but one case this was agreed between the parents.

In one case the mother had sole custody, and in two instances sole custody was granted to the father. In one case joint custody involved shared residence with both parents, and in one some of the children lived with each parent. In five cases no order was made as to the custody of the children. This usually involved older children who were still dependent, often in third-level education. Access was agreed in eight cases, and regulated by an agreed schedule in a further eight. In the one fought case where children were an issue, the schedule formed part of the final order. Access was not specified in 12 of the 29.

Maintenance

Maintenance for children was made an order of the Circuit Court in only half these cases, in nine of the divorces and six of the judicial separations. In two judicial separations maintenance for both wife and children was agreed and made an order of the court. In some cases matters relating to maintenance were referred to the District Court. In others it was not mentioned, suggesting that informal arrangements existed to the satisfaction of the parties. There were three cases, two divorces and one judicial separation, all involving older couples, where maintenance for the wife was made an order as part of the consent.

Family Home

The family home was the other major issue resolved in the finalised cases. In a number of the divorces this had already been disposed of before the divorce application was made. Where the court order makes a consent a rule of court, and this includes formalising the disposal of the family home, this is recorded, even if the disposal took place a year or two previously. In other cases where this occurred some years earlier, with both parties now independently housed, this is recorded either as both having their own homes, or the outcome for the family home not being specified. In seven of the divorces and four of the judicial separations the family home was sold and the proceeds divided between the parties. In some instances the proportions were specified, in others not. In a few instances one party, usually the wife, received more than half the family home in lieu of future maintenance.

In three of the divorce cases it was recorded that both parties now had their own homes. In 10 of the divorces the wife bought out the husband's share, including a few instances where she received it in lieu of future maintenance. This also occurred in five judicial separations. In six divorces, including the two contested ones, the husband bought out the wife's share in the family home. This occurred in one judicial separation. In three divorces and three judicial separations the family home was rented. In eight divorces there was no family home, presumably because the parties had moved on and it had previously been disposed of. In all other cases there was no reference to the fate of the family home.

Financial Orders
Pension adjustment and other financial orders were relatively rare. There were two nominal pension adjustment orders, and four involving the division of the pension or the maintenance of the contingent benefit (death in service benefit) by the wife. There were seven other financial orders, including one in the contested divorce, involving cash sums, land or other property.

Duration of Marriage
Once again, those with marriages of more than 25 years' duration formed the largest group among those divorcing. Fourteen of the divorces involved people who had married between 26 and 30 years previously, followed by nine who had married between 11 and 15 years previously. Seven had been married more than 36 years, seven between 16 and 20 years, five fell into the age-group of those married between 21 and 25 years and three between 31 and 35 years, and three had been married less than 10 years. Again, it must be understood that, given the need for four years' separation and the existence of the remedies of judicial separation and deeds of separation, many of those divorcing had already ended their marriages in all but name, and had resolved most of the issues.

Among those seeking judicial separations, often the first formalised end to a marriage, the age-profile was somewhat different. One couple had been married less than five years, and four between five and 10. Three fell into each of the 11 to 15 and 16 to 20 years' duration of marriage. One couple had been married for between 26 and 30 years, two between 31 and 35 and one over 36 years before seeking judicial separations.

SOUTH-EASTERN CIRCUIT COURTS
The South-Eastern Circuit has a broad geographical spread, stretching from Nenagh on the western end of Co Tipperary to Wexford and Waterford coastal towns, taking in Kilkenny and Carlow. In October 2006 family law hearings took place in Nenagh and Wexford, and 26 cases were heard in all. Of these 22 were consent divorces, of which 14 were preceded by separation agreements or judicial separations. The terms of these were made rules of court in the divorce proceedings. Two judicial separations were granted on consent.

Gender
Women initiated 14 of the divorces and four of the judicial separations, with men initiating eight of the divorces and none of the judicial separations. In all, therefore, women accounted for 18 of the applications, and men for eight.

Type of Application

Two divorce applications were heard, both unusual. In one the only issue being tried was where the applicant wife sought a declaration of an interest in a house owned by the respondent's mother, who was a notice party. This application failed, and the divorce was granted, with costs awarded against the applicant. In the other case a judicial separation had been granted some years earlier, and financial reliefs ordered, but the terms of this had been appealed to the High Court, and the appeal had succeeded, leaving no financial reliefs in place. The applicant husband then sought a divorce. The wife, who practised a very devout form of Catholicism, made no appearance. Buttimer J refused to grant a divorce, as no proper provision had been made for the wife, with none claimed by the wife and none offered by the husband, who had substantial means. This was the only case I observed where a divorce was refused. No heading exists in the Courts Service Annual Reports for divorces refused, so it is not possible to say how often this occurs, but it is likely to be extremely rare or such a category would be created.

Another unusual feature of this group of cases was that in two of the consent divorces the father had sole custody of the children and the mother paid maintenance. In one case the father paid maintenance, but in the majority of cases no maintenance was referred to, perhaps reflecting the fact that such issues had been agreed earlier.

Custody

In 11 of the consent divorce and judicial separation cases there were no dependent children. There were dependent children in 13. In these cases it was agreed that the mother would have sole custody in four of them, the father in two, and joint custody with no primary residence was specified in two. In the four instances in which there was joint custody the children were to reside primarily with the mother in two and the father in two. In one case no custody was specified. In all cases but one access was either as agreed or not specified, and in the single judicial separation case a detailed access schedule was spelled out.

Family Home

In relation to the family home, the husband bought out the wife's share in the majority of cases where it was an issue (seven instances) and in three cases the wife bought out the husband's share. It was ordered to be sold and divided in three cases, though in one of those there was a stay, and the husband was to live in the house until the youngest child was no longer dependent, with the wife paying the mortgage. This was an inverse of the more common outcome, where the wife stays in the family home with the children and the husband pays the mortgage. In one case both parties already had a house, and in eight cases either the family home was rented or there was no reference to it.

Maintenance

Maintenance for children was agreed in three cases, and in two of them, unusually, it was paid to the husband by the wife. As in most other circuits, pension adjustment orders featured only rarely, with one nominal order made. There were two other financial adjustment orders, involving the transfer of land and other property.

Duration of Marriage

As in other circuits, there appeared to be a bulge in those seeking divorces after about 15 years of marriage. The largest group (seven of the 26, with an eighth seeking a judicial separation) fell into this category. Four couples who had married between 11 and 15 years earlier sought divorces, as did the same number who had been married between 21 and 25 years. Two couples married between 31 and 35 years, and one married over 35 years, sought divorces, while one couple sought a judicial separation after this length of marriage. The fact that only two of the 26 were fully contested meant that there was a settlement rate of over 90 percent.

NORTHERN CIRCUIT COURTS

The Northern Circuit encompasses Donegal, Leitrim and Cavan, and in October 2006 24 family law cases were heard in Donegal and Leitrim, of which only five were completed in Leitrim. There was no family law cases heard in Cavan that month.

Only one case went to a full hearing, although three more were due for hearing and were settled on the day of the trial. All of these were in Donegal. This represents a settlement rate of over 95 percent. However, this may be reflective of the type of cases listed that month rather than of the overall trend in this circuit. Two cases—one in each county—concerned declarations of parentage. The remaining 22 contained 18 divorce applications and four applications for judicial separation.

Gender

The four judicial separations were all initiated by women, as were 11 of the divorces. Seven of the divorces were initiated by men.

Type of Application

The one contested case was a divorce application heard in Donegal, involving a couple married between 26 and 30 years, whose family included some still dependent children. In this case custody was awarded to the mother, and maintenance was also ordered. The family home was not an issue.

The judicial separation cases were spread over the age-groups, ranging from one marriage which broke up after less than five years, to one which lasted between 11 and 15 years and one which lasted between 21 and 25 years. All three judicial separations were eventually agreed, and all had dependent children. In one case it was agreed that the mother have sole custody, in another that custody be shared, but with the child or children living with the mother, and in the third that there be joint custody without any such stipulation. In all cases access was agreed. In only one of these cases was the family home an issue, and here it was transferred to the wife in lieu of maintenance.

There were 17 divorces granted by consent, and 12 of them had been preceded by a pre-existing judicial separation or separation agreement, the terms of which were made a rule of court in the divorce.

Custody

Twelve of these cases involved dependent children. It was agreed that the mother have custody in six of them, in another joint custody was agreed with the children living with the mother, joint custody was agreed with no such specification in three, and the father had sole custody in one. No arrangements were specified in one case. In most cases access was as agreed, or not specified.

Family Home

The disposal of the family home only featured in nine cases, probably reflecting the fact that this had been resolved earlier in the course of the separation proceedings. Where it was referred to in the consent divorces it was to confirm an earlier agreement. In four of the nine cases the family home was transferred to the wife on payment of a sum, in one case it was transferred without payment, in another case it was transferred to the husband on his payment of a sum to the wife, and in three cases there was no family home.

Maintenance

Maintenance for the children was agreed in three of the consent divorce cases. There was a nominal pension adjustment order in one, and two other financial adjustment orders, reflecting interests in land or other property.

Duration of Marriage

Those seeking divorces and judicial separations were spread fairly evenly across all age-groups. Four sought divorces after between six and 10 years of marriage, three after 11 or more years, four between 16 and 20, three between 21 and 25 and two couples married between 26 and 30 years. Three couples had been married over 35 years before seeking a divorce. These figures are likely to disguise the fact that many couples, especially those with judicial separations or deeds of separations, may have been living totally separate lives for many more years than the four stipulated in the Constitution and the Act before seeking a divorce.

Among the three couples who sought judicial separations by agreement, one had been married less than five years, one less than 10, and the third between 21 and 25 years.

WESTERN CIRCUIT COURTS

The family law week in October 2006 in the Western Circuit took place in Castlebar, where more than a quarter of the cases went to a full hearing. Thirty-four cases were heard by Groarke J in Castlebar in October 2006, of which 22—less than three-quarters—were settled.

Type of Application

Four cases did not fall under the heading of either judicial separation or divorce: one concerned a HSE application for access to a house to check on the children; another concerned an engaged and cohabiting couple whose house was in their joint names, and who were now separated; another was a case where a divorce had been granted but the financial orders were yet to be made; and the final one was a case where a divorce had been granted but one party was seeking compliance with orders.

Gender

Women accounted for four of the judicial separation applications and 16 of the divorce applications, and men accounted for 10 of the divorce applications and none of the judicial separations. Therefore women applicants outnumbered men by two to one.

Of the 30 cases, six were judicial separations and 24 were divorces. Two of the judicial separations were settled on the basis of consent, and four went to a full hearing. In contrast, 20 of the divorces were settled on a consent basis, of which 13 had been preceded by either a deed of separation or a judicial separation. Four went to a full hearing.

Therefore, 22 of the 30 divorce and judicial separation cases that came before Groarke J were settled, giving a settlement rate of just under 75 percent. This compares with 90 percent in Dublin in the same month, about 86 percent in the South-Western Circuit, and 100 percent in Cork, when all were settled.

However, by isolating one month's cases I am taking a snapshot of family law cases for that period, rather than a random, scientific sample. There may be reasons for clusters of difficult cases in certain months in different circuits, and no conclusions can be drawn from regional variations without a more extensive or more random sampling process.

Children

Children again emerged as a contentious issue. In six of the eight contested cases there were dependent children, compared with only 11 cases among the 22 that were settled. In two of the contested cases the court ruled that the children live with the mother. In the remaining four joint custody was ordered, and in three of them the primary residence was with the mother. The file does not show whether the father had sought sole or shared residency with him. In one of the six there was joint custody and residency.

In the 11 cases involving dependent children that were settled, the mother had sole custody in two, there was joint custody with primary care and control with the mother in three, and joint custody with no residence noted in three more cases. In one case custody was not specified (probably meaning the child, while dependent, was in third-level education and living away from home) and in another some members of the family lived with each parent. In one case the children were all in care.

This shows that where children are a major contentious issue the outcome does not vary significantly between contested and settled cases, suggesting that both the judges and the practitioners operate within certain parameters, set by the right of the child to know and have the society of both parents.

Maintenance

Maintenance was ordered in five of the eight contested cases. In two cases maintenance was ordered for the children only, and in three for both mother and children. In the settled cases maintenance was agreed for the children in three cases, for the wife in one case, and for both mother and children in three. Therefore maintenance was not an issue in five of the 11 settled cases involving children, showing a slightly higher proportion of contested cases where maintenance was an issue.

Family Home

The other major issue dealt with in these cases was the family home. In the 13 cases where there were orders or an agreement following the formalisation of a separation, matters like the family home had usually been dealt with. Therefore it does not always show up in the figures relating to the outcome of the subsequent divorce cases, so there is not a total correspondence between the references to the family home and the total number of cases concluded.

Yet in the majority of cases the wife ended up in residence in the family home, usually buying out the husband's share. This was the outcome in eight of the settled divorces, one of the judicial separations, and in three of the judicial separations that went to a full hearing. In the fourth judicial separation case heard there was no family home.

The husband bought out the wife in three of the settled divorce cases, and the house was sold and divided in one case. In three settled divorce cases and the one contested case, both parties already had houses. In four more cases the couple had lived in rented accommodation.

Financial Orders

The issue of pensions arose quite rarely, being specifically mentioned in only three cases. In one there was a nominal pension adjustment order, in another arrangements were made for the wife to have a share in the husband's pension, and in the third she retained the right to his death-in-service benefit.

Other assets were involved in six of the 30 divorce and judicial separations. In one of the contested divorces, where other matters had been resolved, a further financial settlement was the only issue heard, and the wife was awarded a further small lump sum. In the other cases money, land and property abroad all featured in the final resolution of the case.

Duration of Marriage

As in other areas, marriage breakdown was seen to spread across all age-groups, with a bulge among those married between 21 and 25 years. However, some of this is accounted for by the fact that people in this age-group are now returning to court to obtain a divorce, having had a judicial separation or a separation agreement for years, and now wish to formally end their marriage.

Seven of those couples who divorced by consent had been married between 21 and 25 years, and three couples fell into each of the categories of five to 10 years, 11 to 15, and 16 to 20. Two couples had been married between 26 and 30 years, and two between 31 and 35 years. When the divorces were contested, the picture was somewhat different, with two couples married less than 10 years, one married between 16 and 20 and one over 30 years. The latter case concerned a dispute about property following a lengthy separation.

Predictably, the couples seeking a judicial separation were, on average, married a shorter length of time. Three were married less than 10 years, one less than 15 years, and two less than 20 years.

The picture of family law that emerges from the October 2006 cases in the Western Circuit, as elsewhere, is that the majority of cases are agreed, either by consent following an earlier formalised separation, or where one party has effectively abandoned the marriage and plays no part in the proceedings. Those that are contested usually involve children, maintenance or property, but many of these are eventually resolved. However, based on the files, a few of which date from two, three or more years earlier, there can be a few intractable cases that drag on for years.

Midland Circuit Courts

The Midland Circuit contains the counties of Sligo, Roscommon, Laois, Westmeath and Offaly. In recent years the towns of Mullingar and Portlaoise have expanded as commuter towns, while Sligo, Roscommon and Birr still retain many of the characteristics of local county towns. These factors may influence the character of the family law cases heard in each of them.

Type of Application

In October 2006 family law was heard in Roscommon, Sligo and Portlaoise. Roscommon saw the conclusion of 15 cases, Sligo nine, and Portlaoise 16, a total of 40 in the whole Circuit. In Roscommon there were nine divorces and three judicial separations on consent, and one divorce granted following a hearing. There was one declaration of validity of a marriage and one pension adjustment order. In Sligo there were five divorces granted on consent and one recognition of a foreign divorce, one judicial separation on consent and two maintenance applications. In Portlaoise there were 13 divorces granted on consent, one order made for the County Registrar to sell land following an order in family law proceedings, a District Court appeal, where the decision of the District Court was upheld, and, most unusually, an application to rescind a judicial separation following a reconciliation between the parties.

Of the 40 cases concluded, 33 were divorce or judicial separation applications. Only one of these was fully contested, representing three percent of the total, a settlement rate of 97 percent, though one based on a small sample compared with the Dublin or South-Western Circuits.

Gender
Three of the judicial separations were initiated by women and one by a man, while 19 of the divorces were initiated by the wife, compared with 10 by husbands, giving a total of 11 male applicants as against 22 female.

Duration of Marriage
There were no significant differences between the counties in the length of the marriages brought to an end by judicial separation or divorce. Roscommon saw one marriage ending after less than five years, while there were four across the Circuit ending after 10 years or less. Eleven marriages ended after between 11 and 20 years, and 12 between 21 and 30 years. Four marriages ended after more than 30 years, of which two were marriages solemnised more than 40 years earlier.

Custody
Four of each of the Roscommon and Sligo cases and seven of the Portlaoise cases involved dependent children, a total of 15 or just under half of all cases. In 12 of them joint custody was agreed, in four of which no primary residence was specified. In seven, the child or children's primary residence was with the mother, in one it was with the father. In one case, the contested Roscommon case that went to a full hearing, the father was granted sole custody. In two cases, no order was made as the father was not present in court and he was given notice to make submissions before a final decision was made.

Access was agreed in eight of the cases, and was laid out in a schedule in two. In two of them it was shared equally between the parents, and it was not mentioned in one. In the two cases where the father was not present in court he was also given an opportunity to make submissions on access.

Maintenance
Maintenance was more likely to be agreed or ordered to be paid in Roscommon and Sligo than in Portlaoise. This may indicate that more resources were available in the

families in the rural towns than in Portlaoise, which has many of the characteristics of a commuter town including 20 trains a day to Dublin, five arriving before 9am. The travel time is only 45 minutes, making commuting feasible.

The other towns also saw more assets divided. In the two cases in Roscommon where maintenace was paid the amount fell between €50 and €100 per week per child, and in two cases no maintenance order was made. In Sligo maintenance was agreed at between €50 and €100 in two cases, and in two others it was more than €100 a week per child. In one no order was made.

In contrast, in five of the Portlaoise cases no order for maintenance was made or agreed, and in the two where maintenance was agreed it was less than €30 per week per child. In the remaining two cases issues concerning the children were adjourned until the father, who had not been present in court, had an opportunity to make submissions.

Family Home
The family home was an issue in only a minority of the Roscommon cases, six of the 15. This was because in many of them a previous judicial separation or separation agreement was in place, which had dealt with the family home. It was an issue in seven of the nine Sligo cases and 13 of the 16 Portlaoise ones. The home was transferred to the wife in five of the 26 cases, usually with her taking over the mortgage, though in one it was specified that the husband would continue to pay it. It was transferred to the wife on payment by her of a sum in four cases, and to the husband on him paying a sum in five. In one case the parties' respective shares were agreed, and in four it was agreed that the house be sold and the proceeds divided. In two cases each party had a house when the case was concluded, and in six of them neither owned a house. Five of the cases where neither party had a house were in Portlaoise.

Financial Orders
In four cases—two each in Roscommon and Sligo respectively—land or other financial assets were also divided. A portion of a pension was allocated to the other party in two cases, one each in Sligo and Roscommon, and each centre also saw one nominal Pension Adjustment Order. However, pensions were only an issue in a minority of the cases overall. In Portlaoise there were no cases that month involving assets other than the family home, including pensions. Because only one case was fought to a conclusion in the Midland Circuit in October, it is not possible to comment on any distinction between settled and fought cases in this circuit for this "snapshot" of time.

Overall, the outcomes of the cases in the Midland Circuit seem to indicate the variations in the background and circumstances of the parties. In Portlaoise, which has many of the characteristics of a commuter town, there were fewer claims that month involving the family home, land or other assets than in the two more westerly towns. Maintenance for children was more likely to be ordered or agreed to be paid in Roscommon and Sligo, and was for greater sums when it was ordered than in Portlaoise.

SOME NATIONAL TRENDS

By aggregating these figures, it is possible to discern some national trends. Of all the 511 family law cases heard in the State that month, about 10 percent (52) related to guardianship, paternity, District Court appeals and other matters, leaving 459 judicial separations and divorces.

Females Outnumber Males

Female applicants outnumbered male, but not as dramatically as might be expected from figures in other jurisdictions, where they do so by about two to one (for example, 69 percent of the divorces granted in the UK in 2006 were to women applicants, according to the UK Office for National Statistics, www.statistics.gov.uk).

This may be accounted for by our two-stage process, where most of the reliefs arising from marriage break-up can be, and often are, provided by a judicial separation or a separation agreement, leaving the divorce largely a formality. Among those seeking judicial separation, women outnumbered men significantly, with 76 female applicants compared with 17 male. However, when it came to divorce, the figures were less dramatic, with 171 female applicants as against 133 male. Overall, when both categories of application are combined, there were 247 women applicants and 150 men (not all the files allowed for the gender of applicants to be determined, so the total figure here is less than the total number of judicial separations and divorces above), giving a proportion of 62 percent female applicants as against 38 percent male. As stated above, the proportion of female applicants for judicial separation is significantly greater than for divorce.

Two-Stage Process

The discrepancy between the two kinds of application may be due to the fact that judicial separation is the means whereby various practical and financial reliefs can be found in the immediate aftermath of marriage breakdown. A spouse can seek this remedy after a year's separation, while it is necessary under the Constitution and the 1996 Act to be living separate and apart for four out of the previous five years in order to obtain a decree of divorce. Issues like the custody of children, maintenance for them and the dependent spouse, and the disposal of the family home can be dealt with in a judicial separation. It is not practical for people to have to wait the four years required by divorce legislation to regulate such matters, and the more dependent spouse, usually the wife, will have the more urgent need for such regulation. This is further discussed in Ch. 4.

However, a divorce is most commonly sought when one or other party wants to end the marriage finally and formally, either in order to remarry or to regulate their affairs following a long separation. This is as likely to be an issue for a former husband following marriage breakdown as it is for a wife.

91 Percent Settled

Divorce applications outnumbered judicial separations by more than three to one, with 364 of the former as against 94 of the latter. Only 41, or nine percent, of the cases went to a full hearing. This was twice as likely to be the case when judicial separations were involved as when people were seeking divorces, as 15 out of the 94 judicial separations went to a full hearing (just over 15 percent), while only 26 of the 364 divorces (seven percent) did so.

This is not surprising, as often the contentious issues are sorted out at judicial separation stage, or thrashed out in a separation agreement negotiated by the parties and their lawyers. These then frequently form the basis of a subsequent divorce settlement. While it is not possible to draw definitive conclusions on this, there are some reasons (bolstered by the experience of attendance at court hearings reported in Ch.3) to surmise that divorce has also become the preferred method of legally ending a marriage among those of limited resources, often when the relationship has been over for many years, and there are few financial issues to resolve.

It must also be noted that the settled cases, or consents, and the orders made when judgments are given, do not necessarily indicate the end of the matter. There may be subsequent court hearings to enforce the court orders or the consents that were made a rule of court. The picture that emerges from the consents, however, is one where the parties generally seek a final settlement, except where children are involved, despite the fact that the law keeps the door open for a return to court. The existence of dependent children usually, though not always, means ongoing maintenance and can influence what happens to the family home.

Of the 41 cases that went to a full hearing, 26 involved children—11 judicial separations and 15 divorces. In most of these cases (19) other issues were involved as well, usually the family home and/or maintenance, though the custody of children was the only issue in seven of the 26 cases. In 11 judicial separations and six divorces the family home was an issue, again usually combined with others. In seven judicial separations and 13 divorces other financial matters, either maintenance or the disposal of other properties, were an issue again, often in combination with the issue of children; and there were two cases in which other contentious issues featured (for example, barring orders).

Thus, dependent children featured in 63 percent of the contested family law cases, but in only 37.5 percent of all the cases examined (see below). The family home was an issue in 41 percent of contested cases and maintenance or other financial matters was an issue in 48 percent.

Breakdown Spread Across Age-Groups

A striking feature of the analysis was the extent to which marriage breakdown, or at least the legal end to a marriage, was spread across the age-groups, as indicated by the length of marriages ending in judicial separation or divorce. Because of the two-stage process divorces are more common among the older age-groups. This is because judicial separation is often the first stage of regulating the consequences of the breakdown of a marriage—a solution available a year after the breakdown under the Judicial Separation and Family Law (Reform) Act 1989, with a divorce following later (and only available when the marriage has broken down for a minimum of four years, under the Constitution and the Family Law (Divorce) Act 1996—nonetheless, as the figures above show, both types of remedy are spread fairly evenly across all age-groups.

Only a small number of the files examined showed people seeking a hasty exit from a marriage. There were just 10 applications for judicial separation or divorce (mainly judicial separations) among people married less than five years, just over two percent of the total. However, the figure leaps to 67 among those married between six and 10 years, and there is a further increase among those married 11 to 15 years, where there were 77 applications for judicial separation or divorce. An almost identical number (78) sought this remedy after 16 to 20 years of marriage, and a similar number (75) after 20 and under 25 years. After 25 years of marriage the numbers seeking judicial separation or divorce starts to tail off, with 66 seeking it between 25–30 years of marriage (typically, those in their 50s and early 60s) and 50 seeking it after 30 years of marriage. There were 21 applications from those married between 35 and 40 years, a group typically in their late 60s or early 70s, and six people sought divorces after more than 40 years of marriage. In nine cases the date of the marriage was not stated.

Therefore 230, almost exactly half of all applicants were married between 10 and 25 years when they sought a legal end to their marriages. This group is the most likely to have dependent children, and most of them are also likely to be still paying a mortgage.

Almost a third of all applicants (143) were married for more than 25 years when they applied for judicial separation or divorce. The majority of the applications were for divorce, so it is likely that a significant proportion had been living apart for much more than the requisite four years, and some may already have had judicial separations or separation agreements. From attendance in court and listening to evidence it was clear that this was often the case when older people sought a divorce. According to my observations recorded in Ch.3, when a judicial separation was sought by an older person, however, the marriage had usually broken down quite recently.

Children

Cases involving dependent children made up 37 percent of all the cases examined, that is, 168 cases. However, as we have seen, they made up 63 percent of the contested cases.

Thus issues concerning children in family breakdown situations are among the most contentious.

It is important to state that the files show the outcomes of cases, not the positions taken by people at the initiation of proceedings. It is therefore impossible to know, for example, in what proportion of cases where custody was decided whether one parent sought either sole or joint custody, or whether either parent sought to have the child or children live primarily with him or her, or if they requested to have shared custody. The outcomes show what the result of the proceedings was, not the extent to which one or other party obtained what they were seeking in the teeth of opposition from the other party.

Among the contested cases the mother was granted sole custody in nine cases (33 percent) and the father was granted sole custody in three (11 percent). Joint custody was granted in 14 (52 percent), but in 11 of those (78 percent) the child or children's primary residence was granted to the mother. In the remaining three cases some children were with each parent in one, they shared their residency between both parents in another, and no primary residence was specified in a third. In one family the children were in care.

The pattern is somewhat different among the settled cases. In 29, or 18 percent of the total, it was agreed that the mother have sole custody. It was agreed that the father had sole custody in seven cases, or just over five percent of cases. Thus one or other parent ending up with sole custody was a more likely outcome in contested cases. In 106 cases (66 percent) joint custody was agreed, as compared to it being granted in 52 percent of the contested cases. However, in 63 of these (just under 60 percent) the children's primary residence was agreed to be with the mother, a lower figure than among the contested cases. In 25 no primary residence was specified, most commonly when the children are older or in third-level education. In the remainder residence was shared.

Thus we see that most cases involving dependent children resulted in joint custody being agreed or awarded by the court. However, in the majority of these the primary care and control, or residency, rested with the mother, with the children seeing the father at weekends, either as agreed or according to a schedule which might also include overnight visits during the week and the apportioning of school holidays between the parents. The mother had primary care and control in 70 cases where there was joint custody, the father in five, and it was either shared or some children lived with each parent in 18 cases, with no residence specified in 25.

We find, therefore, that between the mother being awarded sole custody by the court, or this being agreed in a settlement, and her being nominated as the parent with "primary care and control" where joint custody is ruled or agreed, when families break up the children end up living with their mother most of the time in almost two-thirds of the cases. This was the agreed arrangement in 63 percent of the settled cases, with the balance divided among the other categories. This outcome in the settled cases suggests that fathers generally do not seek sole custody or primary care and control when there is joint custody, and the solutions of some children living with each parent, or them sharing their time between the two, were preferred in less than 10 percent of the settled cases.

This could reflect a fatalistic acceptance by fathers that they would not win anyway if the case went to court. However, this is not borne out by the figures, as fathers ended up with sole custody more frequently when cases were contested than when they were settled. It is more likely to reflect the continuing social reality among married couples with children that the father is likely to be the main bread-winner and to work longer hours than the mother, who is more likely to work part-time, if at all. She is therefore more likely to be available to care for the children after school, assuming they are of school-going age.

Parents' Employment Status
This is borne out by the latest figures from the Central Statistics Office, based on the 2006 Census (*Women and Men in Ireland 2006*, CSO, Stationery Office, Dublin). The employment rate of persons aged 20–44 according to family status was seen to vary widely between men and women. The employment rate among men with no children was 94.5 percent and among women with no children was 88.3 percent (CSO, 2006: 14). However, the employment rate among women with children fell sharply, to 58 percent among those with the youngest child under three, 53.5 percent among women with their youngest children between four and five, and 62.6 among women with their youngest child over six. Among men with children in the same age groups the employment rates were 93, 91.9 and 92.9 percent respectively, little different from those for the men with no children.

These figures also show that many of the women who were working were working part-time, as revealed both by their earnings and by the number of hours worked. 79 percent of all women earned less than €30,000 a year (below the average industrial wage), compared with 63 percent of all men (CSO, 2006: 16). These figures do not show the number of hours worked. However, separate figures from the CSO reveal that in 2006, 78.7 percent of men in employment were working 30 or more hours per week compared with 61.2 percent of women (CSO, 2006: 17).

The overall employment rate for women in 2006 was 58.8 percent, of whom 61.2 percent worked over 30 hours a week. This gives us a figure of just under 40 percent of all women working more than 30 hours a week, meaning over 60 percent worked less than 30 hours a week or not at all. As only between 53 and 63 percent of women with young children worked at all, we can assume that the majority of women with young children either did not work or worked part-time. This means they were available to care for their children after school, a more plausible explanation than judicial prejudice for the fact that when families break up the children are more likely to spend most of their time being cared for by their mother.

This trend is also borne out by the ESRI report for the Equality Authority on "Gender inequalities in time use" (McGinnity and Russell, 2008). While it does not examine the numbers of hours worked by women in employment, it examined the time spent on both paid employment and unpaid caring and household tasks by married men and women. Unsurprisingly, it found that women did more unpaid work than men, while men spent longer in paid work, with this increasing sharply among single-earner couples with children (McGinnity and Russell, 2008: xi).

On weekdays women with a youngest child under the age of five spent over eight hours caring for them on weekdays, and almost nine hours caring for them at weekends (McGinnity and Russell, 2008: 38, 39, 40). This fell to just under five hours on weekdays and six-and-a-half at weekends when the youngest was of primary school-age. Men spent about two hours a day with children under five, and less than an hour and a half with children between the ages of five and 10 on weekdays, with this rising to almost three at weekends for younger children and over four when the youngest was of primary school age.

It would appear, therefore, that the division of labour that exists prior to separation is continued in most families post-separation. This may have the effect of disadvantaging fathers in their contact with their children, as in an intact family, even if they spend little time during the working week caring for them, they sleep under the same roof and see the children every day. However, the economics of family life are such that it may be difficult for most couples to alter their working arrangements abruptly when a marriage breaks down.

Joint Custody
Thus, while "joint custody" emerges as the favoured option among both settled cases and those decided by the court, this term hides the reality that children are still more likely to be "primarily resident" with their mother. In a minority of cases sole custody was either agreed to be solely with one parent—and this seemed to be unopposed by the other parent—or this was the decision of the court. In a few cases this appeared to follow allegations of abuse that were substantiated to the court, as indicated by specifications that the father should not have custody even in the event of the death of the mother, but this was rare. On the basis of attendance at court hearings (see Ch.3), I can surmise that usually when one parent became sole custodian this was the result of the other parent having withdrawn from the children's lives, either as a result of addiction or social problems, imprisonment, or having left to form another family. The mother was, or became, sole custodian in 34 cases, and the father in eight.

In four cases none of the above applied, either because the children were in care, or their wishes were specifically referred to.

Maintenance
In most cases where there are dependent children maintenance was agreed by the non-custodial parent, or the court ordered maintenance. The amounts vary, but where these are specified they generally fall within the range of €60–€100 per week per child, along with a share of educational and medical expenses. In cases where the family resources are greater than average, the amount can rise and may include items like boarding school fees.

Maintenance for spouses is infrequent and very rare where there are no dependent children, though there were a few cases where wives in long marriages that came to an end, and who were past working age, received ongoing maintenance. Maintenance is usually paid by the husband though, as seen above, there are instances where the court orders the wife to pay maintenance for the children. Again, the payment of maintenance appears to follow the pre-separation economic relationship, where the husband works longer hours and earns more, and therefore contributes more financially to the family, while the wife spends more time caring for the children.

Family Home
Not all marriages have dependent children but most do, at some stage, have a family home. This featured in 290 of all cases, almost two-thirds, or 63.2 percent. In 49 of these the matter had already been disposed of, or the court made no order in relation to the matter. In 36.8 of cases (169) it did not even feature in the files. In a further 49 cases (out of the 290) it was specified that there was no family home, or it was not mentioned, bringing to a total of 218 the number of cases where there was no family home at issue, a total of 47.5 percent. This left 241 cases where the family home was actually disposed of, or specifically referred to. Therefore it was disposed of by the proceedings in 52.5 percent of the cases.

Where the family home was disposed of, the most likely outcome was that it was transferred to the wife, usually on payment of a sum to the husband and/or with the wife taking on the mortgage. Occasionally the family home was transferred to the wife in lieu, in whole or in part, of past or future maintenance, or against her giving up an interest in other marital property. The family home was transferred to the wife in one of these circumstances in 107 of the 241 cases.

It was transferred to the husband in 41 cases, just under 17 percent of the total. Again, this was usually on payment of a sum to the wife for her interest in it. In 49 cases, or 20 percent of the total, it was agreed or the court ordered that the family home be sold and the proceeds divided between the spouses.

In 24 cases both spouses already had houses, indicating that these proceedings—normally divorce—came years after the marriage had broken down with both spouses already having made arrangements for the rest of their lives. In 10 cases the family home was rented, normally from a local authority. This figure is likely to be under-represented, as the 47.5 percent of cases where the family home was not an issue undoubtedly includes a significant number where one or other or both of the parties live in rented accommodation and had done for a substantial period of time.

There were 10 cases where the issue of the family home fell under another category. This would include, for example, where one or other party had the right to reside in it for specified time, normally until the children were grown up, when it would be sold and the proceeds divided according to proportions agreed or decided by the court, or where both the parties' names were left on it for the foreseeable future, while one party lived in it. Such cases could return to court for further adjudication at a later date.

Other Financial Orders

While the headlines are dominated by "big money" family law cases, with the allocation of substantial sums of money or property from one party to another, in reality in Irish family law this is rare, with most families having very few assets apart from the family home.

In 124 cases orders were made concerning assets other than the family home. This represented 27 percent of all cases disposed of. Of these, one of the main assets is a pension, and Ireland has sophisticated legislation dealing with the allocation of pensions following judicial separation or divorce (Family Law (Divorce) Act 1996). However, only a minority of those seeking judicial separation or divorce avail of it, and even then a significant proportion seek nominal pension adjustment orders, preserving their pensions with the agreement of the other spouse. However, there is no provision for "nominal" pension adjustment orders in the legislation, and their validity remains to be tested. Such a nominal order may be offset against a greater share in the family home, or a share in another family asset. Nominal pension orders were made in 31 cases, or 25 percent of the cases involving other assets, and just under 12 percent of all cases.

In relation to pensions, therefore, there appears to be a reluctance on the part of litigants to exercise their rights under the legislation. This may reflect the age-group most likely to experience marriage breakdown, as over half had marriages between 10 and 25 years old. They may have had more pressing concerns than pensions, notably the issue of the family home and child maintenance, and may have been prepared to barter pension rights in the future for immediate definite gain.

Pension adjustment orders where a portion of the pension, or the contingent benefit (that due to a spouse on the death of the other spouse) was allocated to the other spouse, were made in 39 cases, 31.5 percent of the total cases involving other assets.

Other property was divided in 54 cases, representing 43.5 percent of cases where assets other than the family home were involved, and just over 10 percent of all cases. This normally involved other land or property, or the share in a family business like a public house or farm, or an investment property, or a share in the couple's savings. It is significant, however, that in 73 percent of all the cases disposed of for one month in 2006 there were no assets other than the family home involved in the proceedings.

Overall, the picture that emerges from a survey of the outcomes of family law proceedings in October 2006 is that the vast majority settle eventually by agreement. However, these include those where there are no orders sought or made other than 18(10) orders, extinguishing the parties' succession rights, and those where detailed arrangements are come to involving the custody and maintenance of, and access to, children, the disposal of the family home and of other assets.

Often these issues arise in the same case, where parties seek the assistance of the courts, or their legal advisers, in unravelling a knot of discord that includes the welfare of the children, the disposal of the family home and the regulation of other financial matters. Often again this can go on for years, with some of the cases in the files originating in 2002 or 2003, or even earlier, with multiple motions for discovery, adjournments, interim orders and reports from experts either on child psychology, financial matters, or both.

It is to the live hearing of such cases we must turn to gain some insight into the dynamics of family law in practice.

NATIONAL TRENDS

Figs 1&2: Gender breakdown of applicants

Judicial separations

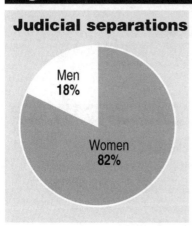

Divorces

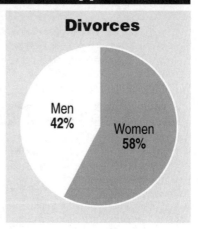

Figs 3&4: Outcomes

Judicial separations

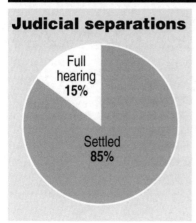

Divorces

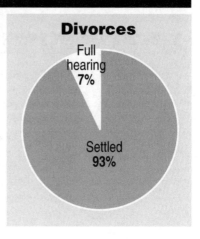

Fig 5: Outcomes relating to children (Total 168)

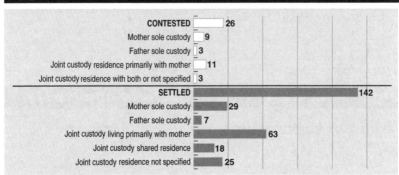

CONTESTED	26
Mother sole custody	9
Father sole custody	3
Joint custody residence primarily with mother	11
Joint custody residence with both or not specified	3
SETTLED	142
Mother sole custody	29
Father sole custody	7
Joint custody living primarily with mother	63
Joint custody shared residence	18
Joint custody residence not specified	25

Fig 6: Cases involving family home (Total 339)

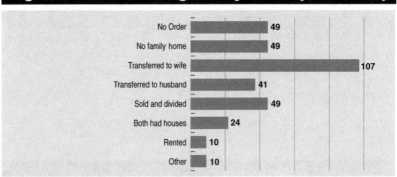

No Order	49
No family home	49
Transferred to wife	107
Transferred to husband	41
Sold and divided	49
Both had houses	24
Rented	10
Other	10

Fig 7: Length of marriage (Total 458)

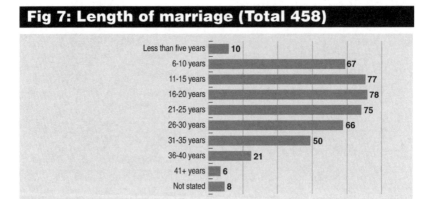

Less than five years	10
6-10 years	67
11-15 years	77
16-20 years	78
21-25 years	75
26-30 years	66
31-35 years	50
36-40 years	21
41+ years	6
Not stated	8

Source: Carol Coulter

Chapter 3

HOW FAMILY LAW WORKS IN PRACTICE

Insights into how family law works in the Circuit Court, where there are virtually no written judgments, can best be obtained by attending at family law cases and observing the hearing of evidence and the making of decisions, particularly on ancillary orders. I will examine here what happened in the various Circuit Courts I attended during the legal year 2006–2007, including, but not restricted to, the making of ancillary orders. I will also look at the extent to which the legislation is referred to in argument before the court and in the making of the orders, especially the conditions spelled out in s 16 of the Family Law Act 1995 and s 20 of the Family Law (Divorce) Act 1996 for the making of orders relating to provision for dependent members of the family, and to case law from the superior courts.

Legislation

The legislation governing the making of ancillary orders is: the Guardianship of Infants Act 1964; the Family Law (Maintenance of Spouses and Children) Act 1976; the Family Home Protection Act 1976; the Family Law (Protection of Spouses and Children) Act 1981, largely superseded by the Divorce Act 1996; the Domicile and Recognition of Foreign Divorces Act 1986; the Status of Children Act 1987; the Judicial Separation and Family Law Reform Act 1989; the Children Act 1989; the Family Law Act 1995; the Domestic Violence Act 1996, and the Family Law (Divorce) Act 1996 (Consolidated).

While a multiplicity of orders can be made under these Acts, in practice a relatively limited number are made in the Circuit Court on a regular basis. These are decrees of divorce and judicial separation and, occasionally, nullity; declarations of parentage, exemptions of the three-months, notice requirement for marriage, and ancillary orders or interim orders relating to three main areas: children, maintenance and other financial matters; and the family home, with domestic violence orders previously made in the District Court occasionally either appealed to the Circuit Court or such orders being sought and incorporated into an overall package of orders made in conjunction with a separation or divorce.

As most of the decrees made in the Circuit Court are divorce decrees, the Family Law (Divorce) Act 1996 is the Act most widely used, followed by the Judicial Separation and Family Law Reform Act 1989. Judicial separations are granted under this latter Act, and may be sought under a number of grounds, but almost always, as the examples below illustrate, they are sought on the ground that:

> "the marriage has broken down to the extent that the court is satisfied in all the circumstances that a normal marital relationship has not existed between the spouses for a period of at least one year immediately preceding the date of the application."
> (s 2(1)(f) of the Family Law Reform Act 1989)

The Act provides for a number of ancillary reliefs, including maintenance, the transfer of property, the payment a lump sum, and arrangements for the custody of and access to the dependent children of the family defined as those under 18, or under 21 if in full-time education (later increased under the Family Law Act 1995 to 23). Many of these provisions are mirrored in the Family Law (Divorce) Act 1996, which also provides for pension adjustment orders.

Much attention has been focused in the superior courts on the "proper provision" requirements of the Constitution and the Family Law (Divorce) Act 1996. The seminal case here was *T v T* [2002] 3 IR 334, when the Supreme Court set out general principles which are applicable in deciding what constitutes "proper provision" in such cases. The evolution of case-law in this area has been tracked by family law specialist Gerry Durcan SC (Durcan: 2007).

Section 20 of this Act (mirroring s 16 of the Family Law Act 1995) stipulates that the court shall "ensure that such provision as the court considers proper having regard to the circumstances exist or will be made for the spouses and any dependent member of the family concerned." In so doing, it shall have regard to the following:

"(a) the income, earning capacity, property and other financial resources which each of the spouses concerned has or is likely to have in the foreseeable future,

(b) the financial needs, obligations and responsibilities which each of the spouses has or is likely to have in the foreseeable future (whether in the case of the remarriage of the spouse or otherwise),

(c) the standard of living enjoyed by the family concerned before the proceedings were instituted or before the spouses commenced to live apart from one another, as the case may be,

(d) the age of each of the spouses, the duration of their marriage and the length of time during which the spouses lived with one another,

(e) any physical or mental disability of either of the spouses,

(f) the contributions which each of the spouses has made or is likely in the foreseeable future to make to the welfare of the family, including any contribution made by each of them to the income, earning capacity, property and financial resources of the other spouse and any contribution made by either of them by looking after the home or caring for the family,

(g)   the effect on the earning capacity of each of the spouses of the marital responsibilities assumed by each during the period when they lived with one another and, in particular, the degree to which the future earning capacity of a spouse is impaired by reason of that spouse having relinquished or foregone the opportunity of remunerative activity in order to look after the home or care for the family,

(h)   any income or benefits to which either of the spouses is entitled by or under statute,

(i)   the conduct of each of the spouses, if that conduct is such that in the opinion of the court it would in all the circumstances of the case be unjust to disregard it,

(j)   the accommodation needs of either of the spouses,

(k)   the value to each of the spouses of any benefit (for example, a benefit under a pension scheme) which by reason of the decree of divorce concerned, that spouse will forfeit the opportunity or possibility of acquiring,

(l)   the rights of any person other than the spouses but including a person to whom either spouse is remarried."

With the exception of sub-clauses (k) and (l), these repeat identical provisions in s 16 of the Judicial Separation and Family Law Reform Act 1989.

Regarding the children, s 5(2) of the Family Law (Divorce) Act 1996 states:

"Upon the grant of a decree of divorce the court may, where appropriate, give such directions under section 11 of the Act of 1964 as it considers proper considering the welfare (within the meaning of that Act), custody of, or right of access to, any dependent member of the family concerned who is an infant within the meaning of that Act as if an application has been made to it in that behalf of that section."

The 1964 Act referred to is the Guardianship of Infants Act 1964 and s 11 provides that any person being a guardian of an infant may apply to the court for directions on any question concerning the welfare of the infant, and the court can gives directions concerning custody of, access to and maintenance of the infant. Sections 41 of both the Judicial Separation and Family Law Reform Act 1989 and the Family Law (Divorce) Act 1996 Act provide that the court may, when granting a decree of divorce, declare that either of the spouses concerned is unfit to have custody of any dependent member of the family who is a minor.

The operation of the whole of the Family Law (Divorce) Act 1996, including the granting of ancillary orders, in the light of the developing jurisprudence of the superior courts has been fully examined by Geoffrey Shannon in *Divorce Law and Practice*, published by Thomson Round Hall (Shannon, 2007). However, due to the virtually total absence of written judgments in the Circuit Court, his analysis was generally unable to include rulings from this court. The cases described below represent a selection of those where the court made rulings on ancillary orders, interim orders or where there were appeals of decisions of the District Court.

62 Days in Courts

I attended 19 courts in all across the eight Circuits, spending a total of 62 days in court. In some of the courts the resident Circuit Court judge presided, in others it was one of the moveable judges, who therefore sometimes presided in more than one Circuit. During the time I was present 349 matters came before various Circuit Courts. Of these 26 were District Court appeals, five were issues relating to non-marital children, 10 came under the heading of "other" including matters like dispensing with the permission of a parent for a passport, and 44 were interim matters while divorce or judicial separation proceedings were ongoing or ancillary matters requiring further attention from the court following the making of a decree of divorce or judicial separation. Twenty-five applications or motions were adjourned. This left 239 judicial separation and divorce cases that were concluded in my presence.

The total number contested came to 43. Six of the judicial separations and three of the divorces were settled after a hearing, sometimes one going on for days, while there were 187 cases where the parties had settled all issues and came to court to have the case ruled and the decree issued. These included, on the one hand, cases that came to court requiring no orders to be made other than that extinguishing succession rights, and on the other those that followed negotiations between the parties, usually with legal representation, and a settlement required to be made a rule of court.

The settlement rate of these cases therefore came to 82 percent, which is lower than that observed from the "snapshot" of cases concluded in all the circuits in October 2006. This can be explained from the fact that the days I attended were not fully representative. If there was a family law week in a given Circuit and a day of it was being given over to consent divorces awaiting ruling, as was often the case, I did not attend for that day, as it would not yield any new information on the processing of family law applications. Therefore the number of consents is under-represented in these figures, and it is reasonable to surmise that if the consents from these days were added in that the settlement rate would resemble closely that of the October 2006 sample.

The other interesting figure that emerges from this, and which is absent from the figures from the October 2006 files, is the number of interim applications, or issues returning to court following a final ruling on a judicial separation or divorce. There were 44 such cases, representing 13.5 of all the cases heard, excluding the adjournments. Such applications are the hallmark of very contentious cases, and also indicate the lack of finality in the Irish family law regime. I will return later to the subject matter of such applications.

Among the settled cases there were 49 divorce applications where it was stated that there was a judicial separation or separation agreement in existence, and the terms of this were made a rule of court when the decree of divorce was issued. However, in 104 of the divorces, twice that number, there was no previous judicial separation or separation agreement. There were 34 judicial separations on consent.

Of the contested cases, 23 were judicial separations, while 20 were divorces. Given that there were 57 judicial separations in all, this shows that 40 percent of those I witnessed were contested. In contrast, only 20 of the 173 divorces were contested, representing only 11.5 percent. As I pointed out above, this is probably an overestimation of the number contested, given that I was not present for all consents during each family law session, so an even higher proportion of divorces were uncontested.

Clearly, therefore, judicial separation proceedings are more contentious than divorce proceedings. This is not surprising, as judicial separation proceedings are normally taken in the immediate aftermath of the breakdown of a marriage, when one or other of the parties wishes to sort out matters relating to children, the family home and financial matters. Further, in a handful of the judicial separation cases I attended the issue of fault was raised, when emotions were still clearly raw arising from the breakdown of the marriage. Because divorce can only be sought after the couple has lived apart for a minimum of four years out of the past five, many of these issues are usually resolved by the time the matter comes to court.

Children emerged as by far the most contentious issue, with 73 of the District Court appeals, interim matters or contested applications featuring issues to do with custody of and access to children. This could be combined with other issues—maintenance featured in 38 of the cases. The family home was the contentious issue in 33, though this too was sometimes combined with other issues. Among older parties, however, it was often the only issue. The conduct of one or other of the parties was a major feature of three cases, including two where the cases were settled after a long hearing.

I will now look at the contentious issues as they were treated in different cases and by different courts, based on a selection of cases. I am not examining every contested case. Some of them were very repetitive in the issues raised and the way in which they were dealt with, with extensive examination of bank accounts which ultimately decided very little, or disputes about custody or access that revealed more about the level of hostility between the parents than any developments in judicial decision-making in relation to children. That said, each case is different, with different circumstances, so comparisons will always be difficult. Nonetheless, some trends can be discerned from the cases that were heard. All of the cases are described in accordance with the Protocol for the protection of the anonymity of the parties appended to this work, and they have been reported in *Family Law Matters* (Coulter (ed.), 2007).

I have selected for examination 12 cases concerning children. The selection was made based on their representative nature both geographically and in terms of the issues raised, type of relief sought and reasons for the judicial decision taken. I have selected 10 cases concerning maintenance or other financial issues, and nine concerning the family home, again, choosing them on the basis of the legal issues raised, their representative nature both socially and geographically, and their spread across different circuits and judges. I describe three cases where conduct was raised as a central issue.

CHILDREN
Case Study 1
The first case I will examine concerned a married couple who had not yet finalised their separation, but where the District Court had ordered an interim arrangement concerning their four-and-a-half year old daughter, whereby she spent alternate weeks with each parent. This followed a s 20 report from the social services, where, at the request of the court a social worker saw the family and the child in order to inquire into her welfare and best interests. The mother, who was from Eastern Europe, lived with her mother and the mother's partner, and the household also contained a lodger. These living arrangements may have reflected a greater acceptance by the mother than the father of living in a large family group. The father lived alone, but had an older son from a previous relationship whom he saw regularly.

The mother came to court in the Midland Circuit seeking a change in the arrangement, whereby the child would stay with her during the week and see her father at weekends. The father opposed this. He was suffering from depression due to the breakdown of his marriage, and was on a back-to-work scheme, but tailored his hours in order to be able to collect his daughter from school on the week she stayed with him. The mother was working, and her mother looked after the child when she was at work.

At an early stage in the case Murphy J said:

> "What is decided today may not be the right solution in two, three or four years' time. Things evolve. The issue is, where is she during the school-going week, that is, Sunday night to Thursday night? It is probably better regarding the future if she is in the same house every night. The days of children playing in the street are gone. They are in each other's houses. It is preferable if they are in the same house every week. It provides an element of consistency in relation to homework etc. The social worker's report had no fundamental objection to any arrangement. If something could be arranged by consent it would be very desirable. Surely the father's ambition is to return to work full-time?"

He asked the parties to consider what he had said over lunch, and attempt to reach agreement. No agreement was reached, and the case continued with evidence.

The husband gave evidence concerning his working hours and his house, including photographs of it. He said that his wife did not look after the child, it was her mother who did so. He was concerned about the grandmother's boyfriend, who he claimed was an alcoholic. He said his daughter said she did not have her own room in the house, and had told him of fighting incidents in the house. "As a father I should have more entitlement to be there than the granny," he said. He was also concerned that the mother now had a boyfriend whom she was bringing back to the house.

The judge asked him: "Are you giving too much of yourself to the child rather than devoting yourself to getting back to work?" The father responded: "How can you ever be too much devoted to your own child?" This exchange reflected the fact that the judge's assumption was that the father's intention—and perhaps duty—was to return to work full-time, leaving the mother as the primary carer. As is shown by the CSO figures cited in Ch.2, this reflects statistically the most common situation, but it does not necessarily reflect the wishes of all fathers.

It emerged that relations between the father and the grandmother were poor, but he told the judge he would seek to improve them for the sake of the child.

The mother gave evidence that she thought it was in the daughter's best interests to have a single base. "A week is a long time for a child. She comes home upset. Loads of times she says she doesn't want to go. I stay with her till she falls asleep. He wants to make a four-year-old act like an adult." She acknowledged she was now in a new relationship, but said that this did not affect her parenting. She also denied her mother's partner was an alcoholic.

After listening to the evidence, Murphy J gave the following orders:

1   there would be joint guardianship and custody of the child;
2   the child was to stay in Ireland unless both parents agreed in writing that she could go abroad;
3   custody arrangements were to stay as they were with the following modifications: the non-custodial parent would have access to the child every Wednesday from the end of school until 7pm, the non-custodial parent would have access from 5pm on Christmas Eve until 12 noon on Christmas Day, and on the child's birthday the non-custodial parent would have access from 2pm until 6pm.

There was to be liberal access by phone at all times to the absent parent. While the child was in the mother's house she was not to sleep in a room with any man. On the first Saturday of every month at 10am both parents and the grandmother were to meet for half an hour to arrange matters and ensure there were ongoing cordial relationships. The child's passport was to be retained by the District Court, which was to hear any further applications relating to custody and access.

While adjourning another case in that family law week Murphy J remarked: "The norm is, joint guardianship and joint custody, with primary care and control to the mother." Again, as we have seen from the outcomes and CSO statistics in Ch.2, this reflects the imbalance in working hours and earning powers between the majority of spouses.

From his early remarks in this case, this was Murphy J's inclination at the outset of the case. However, as he listened to the evidence he came to the view that the existing arrangements, with the modifications outlined above, were the best solution in this situation. The modifications are all aimed at ensuring the child did not feel cut off from the non-custodial parent in the week she was with the other parent, and that good relations were fostered between her three carers, mother, father and grandmother. It is significant, in my view, that the father's working arrangements were sufficiently flexible for him to be with the child after school.

Case Study 2

In a case on the Eastern Circuit a woman who was a recovering alcoholic sought access, including overnight access, to her daughter, aged eight, who was living with her father. This was opposed by the child's father, because on previous occasions the child had been left alone when the mother was drinking. The mother had two sponsors from Alcoholics Anonymous with her in court.

After listening to evidence from one of the AA sponsors, McCartan J said:

> "Ms F (the sponsor) impresses me. I can understand the apprehension of [the father]. [The wife] fell off the wagon and the child ended up in a police station. She seems a very resourceful and articulate child. What I would propose is that if she met Ms F her worries might be allayed. I would suggest the next two meetings should be with Ms F. [The mother] must realise the more she is intoxicated the more damage is done. I wouldn't expect a child to be about someone who is drinking. Start with Saturdays from 2–5pm with Ms F in the family centre. There is no impediment to you making your own arrangements."

The case illustrates the fact that a parent's addiction can be a major element in court decisions concerning custody and access as it affects parental capacity, one of the criteria considered in determining welfare.

Case Study 3

In another case on the same circuit an unmarried father who had weekend access to his three teenagers, two boys and a girl, had obtained a District Court order to have custody of the two boys, claiming that this was what they wanted, while the custody of the girl remained with the mother. The mother, a non-Irish national, appealed. While giving evidence the father acknowledged that he did not speak to the mother.

McCartan J heard evidence from both parents, and also saw the boys in his chambers at lunchtime. Following this, he made the following ruling:

"This is an appeal against a ruling of the District Court. I have listened to the parents. It is terribly tragic that they cannot find the means to behave civilly towards each other. Do you ever stop to think of the example you are giving? You are the models for your children. You cannot find it in yourselves even to refer to each other by first names. The pair of your should be ashamed of yourselves.

What example are your children going to follow when they go out into the world? Into relationships? How can they talk to their friends about their mum and dad? It must be agony for them when they see their friends' parents getting on. Relations break down. People move on in their lives. After four years there should be a capacity to put the children in the frame.

You [the mother] asked for experts. They don't need them. Your children are beautiful, intelligent, healthy children. What's going down deep is that they're hurt and confused.

For the past four years they have been living in [this town] and have a regular cycle in their lives. [The father] has a view that things would be better for the boys if this changed. I have talked to the children. I would not be disposed to move them until at least the Junior Cert is over. I will leave it as it is, with regular visits to [their father] at weekends. What the children said to me in my room I said would remain confidential. But I am satisfied that the decision I am making will not upset any of them unduly. In a few years I will revisit the issue. Where there is a doubt it is better to leave things as they are. They are beautiful children. They are not unhappy. I want to make it clear that [their father] has as much right to be involved in their lives as [their mother] has."

This was one of the few cases where the judge sought the views of the children in his chambers, and a number of judges indicated their willingness to do so when the children were of a sufficiently mature age. However, certain judges do not hear children, even adult children, either in their chambers or in court, on the basis that this would make the discord between the parties even greater and cause further distress to the children. The question of the right of children to be heard in legal proceedings concerning them, likely to become a live issue through EU law, which requires that children have an opportunity to be heard in relation to proceedings concerning them in accordance with their age and maturity (see Shannon, 2007: 250–251 for a discussion of Brussels II bis in this regard), was scarcely discussed in any of the cases I attended, and may await a ruling from the superior courts.

Case Study 4

In a case before Dublin Circuit Court a divorce application was made, following a judicial separation. The father sought permission to take his two sons, aged seven and 10, on overnight visits to his own father, who lived outside Dublin. Minor issues relating to the family home and maintenance were also being tried. The husband had previously had legal representation, but now represented himself as he could no longer afford it.

He said in evidence that allegations had been made that his father had abused both him as a child, and the children, one of whom had special needs. The allegation was investigated by the health board and considered to be unfounded, but his father was unable to see the children for a while, and he could not take them to see him for weekends. The man was in his 70s and suffered from a heart condition.

In her evidence the wife said that one of the children in question needed routine because of his special needs. A letter had been received from the school which described inappropriate behaviour on his part toward other boys, giving rise to the allegation of abuse. It was difficult for the health board to investigate it because of his syndrome. She was still unhappy about overnight access in the grandfather's house.

In his ruling McMahon J said:

> "I would like to emphasise that the differences between the parties are not great. They have addressed the problems that followed from their unhappy differences. The only issue at stake is the access to the grandfather. You have worked out access between yourselves in an admirable fashion. You have a basic respect for each other and the other's position. This is positive for the children and especially for the difficult position of the older boy.
>
> In relation to access there is no proof before this court of any wrong-doing on the part of the grandfather. I saw the letter from the health board who stopped investigating it. But it is clear the wife has fear and apprehension, though it is not evidence-led. Even if it is irrational I must respect it. While she is of this frame of mind it would be disproportionate of me to order an overnight. I would be doing more harm than good.
>
> I know this will be hard on the husband. But summer is coming up, with long evenings to make the trip [to the grandfather's house]. I know from my own experience that the tolerance of a 75-year-old for young children is not great. I am not condemning anyone here. Access will be as agreed between the parties except for no overnight access with the grandfather."

In this case the judge's concern was clearly for the psychological and emotional welfare of the mother, while attempting to balance this with the legitimate wishes of the father.

Case Study 5

A District Court appeal of an access order took most of a day in Cork. The case concerned an unmarried couple, who had two daughters, aged eight and four. On their separation they had initially agreed that the children share their time equally with both parents, staying half of each week with each, seven nights out of every 14 on a five-week rota. The father was a self-employed consultant while the mother worked in a large organisation.

Subsequently the mother moved with the children to a town about 60 miles from Cork, changing their school. The father challenged this in the District Court, which ruled that they continue to live in this town, with weekend access for the father on three weekends a month, and one evening a week, also in the town. This was reduced to two weekends a month on appeal from the mother to the District Court. The father was now appealing the District Court ruling to the Circuit Court, seeking the return of the children to Cork.

He gave evidence of being the primary carer of the children when they were young, and of caring for them half the time since the separation from the mother. He said he took them swimming, entertained their friends in his home, where he had a trampoline for them, and that they were very happy in Cork. They were now being looked after during the day by an au pair from Eastern Europe. Their mother was still working in Cork and was away for about 12 hours a day. If the children moved back to Cork their mother could see them after school, and at weekends take them to this other town every second weekend and bring them back on Monday morning.

The mother gave evidence that she had had decided to move to the other town, where several members of her family lived, when her sister developed cancer. The children had their extended family there. The au pair was in the house when the mother left in the morning, and the au pair got the children up and out to school. She did their homework with them in the evening. She (the mother) got home about 7pm, occasionally later. She said she was looking for a job locally. She said that as a single mother she needed the support of her extended family.

Kenny J asked her if she was in a relationship, and she said she was not. Asked about her plans for a relationship in the future, she said the matter did not arise. Judge Kenny adjourned the hearing for 40 minutes while he considered the matter. On his return he said:

> "The children will remain with their mother in [the town]. I accept both parents have a very good relationship with the children. I have given very serious consideration to placing the children with their father. But the mother's willingness to work locally has tipped the balance, hence the urgency of her getting a job locally.

The father will have weekend access every second weekend in [the town] from 10 am on Saturday to 6pm on Sunday. He can elect to have the children with him in Cork every two months, from 4pm on Friday to 6 pm on Sunday. The mother will vacate the house on the weekends the father is there. The parties must exercise civility towards each other.

The mother is the primary carer. There is joint custody. Both parents are to be present at First Communions and Confirmations and ceremonies in schools.

There are to be no male visitors at night in the house in [the town]."

He said he would review the matter two months later. In fact, before the case came before him for review the parties negotiated a settlement which varied the orders made.

This was the first case I heard where the court reduced the amount of time a father spent with his children when he previously had an equal share in their care, and where the mother was then defined as the primary carer in opposition to the wishes of the father. As Kenny J never got to review the case because it was settled, we cannot know what the outcome of this review might have been, especially if the mother had failed to obtain work locally.

Case Study 6
An access dispute on the Western Circuit concerned a two-and-a-half year old child, whose unmarried parents each cared for her half the time, according to a District Court ruling that she was entitled to unrestricted access to both her parents. This had followed Section 20 reports on the parents and child carried out by social workers. The father had gone to court because he wanted to take her to the UK to see his mother, but the child's mother opposed the visit. The father was not in court, but was legally represented, as was the mother.

Asked why she did not want the child going to the UK, she said she was worried about the care the child received with her father. She claimed that the child came back from visits to him and his partner and their other children not very clean and sometimes wearing boys' clothes. He also refused to feed the child the special formula milk the mother had chosen for her. He had threatened to take the child out of the jurisdiction and not bring her back. She was concerned that if the child, who suffered from chest infections, became ill the father would not take her to a doctor. She also said she was not happy with the level of access ordered by the District Court and was appealing it, and she gave various reasons why.

Giving his decision, McDonagh J said there was just one issue to be decided here: the trip. It would be decided on the balance of probabilities. "I will not permit the child to be taken out of the country by [her father]. Every other aspect of access is to be unchanged until the full hearing of the appeal. Both parties should bring a bit of realism into this as well," he said, without elaborating further.

Again, the court maintained the status quo while awaiting a full hearing on all the issues.

Case Study 7
In a case on the South-Western Circuit O'Donohue J was asked to adjudicate on whether a 12-year-old boy, the older of two, could go to boarding school, as his mother wished, or should attend the local secondary school, in line with his father's wishes. The couple had a judicial separation. The father pointed out that his access would be affected if the boy went away, as he would only see him every six weeks. His mother felt strongly this school was best for him, and her brothers had attended it. She was in a new relationship, and was willing to pay the fees.

After hearing the views of both parties, O'Donohue J said he would adjourn the matter and talk to the boy privately to ascertain his wishes. He ordered both parties to refrain from discussing it with him, and the mother to produce tangible evidence of how she was going to fund the fees, if he decided the boy should go to boarding school.

When the case came back before him, he said the boy could attend the boarding school for a year, on the basis that the mother would pay for it, and he would review the matter then. He increased the father's access during school holidays to compensate for the time he lost as a result of his decision.

The interview with the child was again clearly a crucial element in his decision. The fact that the case was to be reviewed in a year illustrates the fact that cases concerning custody and access are interlocutory and can be reviewed at any time in the light of changing circumstances, and the courts use this facility.

Case Study 8
Access was again in dispute in a District Court appeal before Buttimer J in the Eastern Circuit. The parents were unmarried. The District Court had ordered that the father could have supervised access to his five-year-old son, supervised by the child's grandfather. According to the mother he had not kept to the terms of the access, he had threatened members of her family, he was violent and she wanted access discontinued. The father said he was attending a parenting course, and alleged that his partner had left the child with drug dealers. He said he had cooperated fully with the HSE.

Buttimer J ruled that supervised access should continue, with nominated supervisors, stressing that the father should be reminded of what supervised access meant. "Access is the right of the child," she commented, a view she repeated in a number of such cases before her. This reflects Irish and ECHR case law, as outlined in Shannon (2007: 233–236).

Case Study 9

Buttimer J heard another case where interim access was at issue pending the outcome of a judicial separation. The father wanted shared custody of the two children, while the mother wanted them at home on school nights. Buttimer J said that they should work out a schedule for the summer holidays. Then the children should be with their father from Thursday through Saturday, and if that worked, increase it. She said she was trying to facilitate them staying in the same bed on school nights, that is, from Sunday until Thursday.

Again, she indicated that the arrangement could be reviewed in the light of experience.

Case Study 10

A District Court appeal in Dublin concerned an 18-year-old mother's application for access to her eighteen-month-old son. The District Court had given sole custody and primary care and control to the child's father. The couple, both young, were unmarried. The District Court had not mentioned access, which the mother was now seeking. Neither was legally represented.

The mother told the court that the couple had broken up about six weeks after the birth of the child because the child's father was hitting her, and she went back to her mother. She had post-natal depression, which was undiagnosed. She was now living with her grandfather and her aunt, and was working, earning €600 a week. The father had applied to the District Court for sole custody, which she did not contest as she did not appear in court, claiming she was afraid of the father. She said the social worker had told her she should have the child on Fridays. She said she would like joint custody.

The child's father said when the child was born the mother did not want anything to do with him. She was out all the time. He said he had to collect the child numerous times from the child's grandmother's. The mother came to him at work and left the child with him sopping wet. She was financially irresponsible. He said he had spoken to her parents who said they were worried about her, her whereabouts and her behaviour. If she had access to the child it would be taken from her as she was not a suitable carer.

He said he was living with his parents and five brothers, and had his own room which he shared with the baby. He was 21. He was in FÁS completing his Leaving Certificate. He was in a stable relationship and was going to get engaged. He would be able to take care of the child. Asked if the child should not see his mother, he said she had been seeing him, but was out drinking all the time, had been out bouncing cheques and he did not want the child exposed to her lifestyle, being old enough now to remember things.

Judge McDonagh said that as an interim measure he was going to allow access. He thought both should be legally represented and should apply to the Legal Aid Board. In the interim he was going to allow supervised access in the mother's grandfather's house every Saturday from 11am until 7pm, and either the grandfather or the aunt would have to be there at all times. In the meantime custody and primary care and control should remain with the father, affirming the District Court order. Both parties should get legal advice and come back with social workers' reports, he said.

The case illustrates the reliance that judges placed on reports from social workers. It also demonstrates the fact that mothers cannot expect automatic custody, or primary care and control, especially if they demonstrate any issues with alcohol or drug abuse.

Case Study 11

Another District Court appeal came before McDonagh J, where the District Court had ordered that the access take place in what had been the home of a formerly engaged couple, who had two children, aged eight and six. This meant that the mother had to leave the house while the father spent his access time, from Sunday to Tuesday, with the children. The house was in the couple's joint names, and partition proceedings had been served. The mother sought a variation of the access order, saying she found it unworkable.

She said the children were allowed to stay up too late, there was no routine, the house was not left as she wished, housework was not done, and there was evidence of smoking in the house. She thought access should take place in the father's mother's house, but this would have to be at weekends, as the children had to go to school, and the mother's house was too far away. The husband's barrister said that his mother's house was not available for access. The children's mother wanted him out of the house. When he stayed in the house the mother's bedroom was locked and he stayed in one of the children's rooms, while they slept in bunks in the other bedroom.

McDonagh J said that the property issues had been left unresolved for two years. A defence and counter-claim on this issue had to be served within a week, and it could be six months before there was a hearing date. In the meantime a schedule should be written out in relation to the children's time for getting up, meals, homework and bed-time. The house should be left spick and span. There should be no smoking whatsoever in the house, as one of the children had asthma, and the children's welfare must be paramount. The other party must not visit the area around the house while the resident party was in it. This regime was to continue until the partition proceedings, which should be expedited. "This has nothing to do with the children," he commented. "This is about property, about control."

His comments illustrate the fact that in many cases there are multiple issues which are entangled, and where one issue may be used to prosecute another. It raises the question as to whether issues relating to children should be dealt with in an autonomous manner in family law proceedings.

Case Study 12
A case in the South-West concerned both the family home and two dependent children, both teenage boys. The older one was living with the father in the family home and the younger with the mother, but he spent weekends with his father. The mother was living with her female partner, and the father said that the children were very unhappy about this. The older one did not speak to his mother and the 13-year-old wanted to live with him but, because of the father's work situation, he could not have the younger one live with him during the week.

The solicitor for the mother said that she wanted joint custody, with one child living with each parent, and access to the other parent. She was also looking for a lump sum in compensation for leaving the family home. The husband said he had already paid her €15,000 for her interest in the family home, and could not afford any more. O'Donohue J ordered that she receive a third of the value of the equity in the family home, that there be joint custody of the two dependent children with one continuing to live with each parent. If the husband could not raise the money within two years, the family home was to be sold and the proceeds divided according to his ruling.

His ruling on custody and access demonstrates the fact that, while a parent's sexual orientation may cause discomfort to a teenage child, this is not a basis on which the court will decide custody or care and control. While ECHR jurisprudence exists on this issue (*Da Silva Mouta v Portugal* [1999] EHRR 176 9, December 21, 1999, *EB v France*, Application No. 43546/02 22 January 2008), this was not referred to by either party or by the judge during the hearing. He also did not seek the views of the child, who was a teenager and whose views should have been considered if the child so wished, even if they were not determinative.

MAINTENANCE AND OTHER FINANCIAL MATTERS
When District Court appeals are removed from the total number of cases dealt with by the Circuit Court, maintenance and financial issues rival those related to children in terms of causing friction between former spouses, or the non-marital parents of children. The fact that sometimes the amounts involved could be very small did not diminish their importance for the parties.

Case Study 1
A case on the Northern Circuit heard by O'Hagan J concerned arrears of maintenance owed by a separated man to his wife and mother of his four dependent children, along with an application from him that he reduce his maintenance from €250 a week to €150. While

at this stage his only income was a social welfare payment, he had received a redundancy payment of €44,000 and owned two houses and three other parcels of land. Much of the redundancy money had been spent, but some remained in a bank account. Most of the land had been sold for €300,000, which he had not yet received. Under a separation agreement, one of the houses was to be transferred to the wife, mortgage-free, and he was to keep the other. He had not been paying the mortgage on the family home due to go to his wife.

After hearing evidence O'Hagan J said:

> "I have in mind not to vary the €250 a week maintenance, but that €150 should be paid until the sale of the land is through. Then the entire of arrears are to be discharged. €2,250 is to be paid immediately out of his bank account. I will return to this issue at the next family law session and consider a lump sum order out of the proceeds of the sale of land at that stage."

He indicated that he was considering calculating what the total amount of maintenance would be until the youngest child reached the age of 18, and make a lump sum order accordingly. This was clearly due to the fact that the man had shown little willingness to comply with the existing maintenance agreement, and an irresponsibility with regard to money, and the judge was clearly inclined to think that the only way of guaranteeing the payment of the money was via a lump sum in advance.

Case Study 2
In a different court on the Northern Circuit an elderly woman sought a lump sum to enable her to buy a modest dwelling. The couple had married in 1959 and had had five children, all now grown up. When they separated the husband remained in the family home, and farmed land worth between €280,000 and €440,000. He also drove a new Mercedes car. His wife was living in rented accommodation on €812 a month social welfare. After an adjournment for discussions, the husband agreed to sell some of his land to pay his wife €225,000 in a lump sum in lieu of arrears of maintenance and for her interest in the family home.

After hearing the evidence O'Hagan J said:

> "Mrs … is away from home for a very long time, and has received very little support. Mr … is in the family home leading a normal life and getting the benefit of the farm. He also enjoys a good car. The parties are in the autumn of their years and matters need to be put in order. The money is to be paid within four months unless the parties agree."

Case Study 3
In a case in Dublin before McMahon J the parties had a judicial separation and the husband was now seeking a divorce. However, the wife said that the maintenance for

the three children of €1,000 a month under the judicial separation had not been paid. Asked why he did not pay it, the husband said he paid the youngest child's school fees and gave the children about €100 a week directly. "Why do you not pay it to your wife?" asked Judge McMahon. "They could spend it on sweets or worse." The husband claimed he was giving the children €700–€800 a month in pocket money.

Asked for pay slips to indicate his income, he said that he could offer a P45. "That's when you're fired," McMahon J said. The man said his employer paid him in cash. McMahon J said that all documents relating to his income were to be with the wife's solicitors within three weeks, and he would hear the case in a month, and in the meantime he was to pay to his wife the money he claimed he gave directly to the children. In another case on the Eastern Circuit, McCartan J stated that pocket money was not "proper provision", and offering pocket money to children in lieu of maintenance did occur in a number of cases across the circuits.

Earlier McMahon J had refused to hear a case because there were no up-to-date affidavits of means. This illustrates the importance of documentary evidence in all cases concerning disputes about maintenance.

Case Study 4

A highly contentious case was heard over a number of separate days by Reynolds J on the Midland Circuit. There were four children of the marriage, and allegations of violence from both parties. The mother alleged that her eldest son had assaulted her, provoking physical rows involving several members of the family. There were three properties in the family—the family home and two investment properties in the rural town. The wife claimed that money from land she had inherited, a total of €400,000, went into the family home and her husband's business. Her husband's barrister claimed that she had squandered most of the money, suggesting that the total amount of money she had invested in her husband's businesses was €120,000. She insisted it was more. She was now looking for a substantial lump sum. The husband said he wanted one of the investment properties, which he had inherited from his father, to go to the eldest son, who lived with him, in accordance with his father's wishes.

The median net valuation on the properties, after liabilities, was €1,325,000, of which the wife was seeking half. The husband said he was unable to raise that sum, and also referred to his wife's conduct as a factor to be taken into account, though this was not pursued during the hearing.

Reynolds J ruled that the wife should have a lump sum of €662,500 to enable her to buy a home for herself and the children living with her, and have a fresh start. She also ruled that the husband should pay €120 a week in maintenance for the children. "I also order costs against the respondent because it will take all of the lump sum to make a fresh start and also there are four dependent children to be taken into consideration," she said.

Here the money inherited by the wife along with her contribution to the family home appeared to influence the outcome of the case.

Case Study 5

A maintenance claim was taken by an 18-year-old girl against her father in a court on the Western Circuit, before McDonagh J. The girl's parents had separated and her mother had died. The girl sued for maintenance by a next friend while still a minor and maintenance orders were in place. She was now doing a post-Leaving Certificate course and was seeking €5,000 lump sum from her father to help support her for the year. An order was in existence to support her while she was in third-level education, but the course was not strictly third-level, and therefore did not meet the criteria of the order (though this is not specified in the legislation, it was in the order by agreement following the previous hearing).

The barrister for the father said that this was not a black and white situation. The father was in a new relationship and had two young children. The girl was receiving €3,500 from a trust fund set up for her following her mother's death. She was also in receipt of a grant. She had received €3,500 from her father. There was no proof she was doing a third-level course. The father could afford maintenance, but not a lump sum. The judge said that the order from the previous July still stood. The girl would be due €5,000 in September if it was confirmed she had a place at third level.

This case demonstrates the fact that a dependent child can seek maintenance on his or her own account if not living with a parent, following a separation and maintenance orders.

Case Study 6

A case in the South-Western Circuit before Keys J, which did not conclude, illustrated the kind of property issues that arise in contentious cases. A couple had separated in 1998 and had a separation agreement. The wife now wanted a divorce and to finalise financial matters. An order had been granted restraining the husband from disposing of property and freezing his assets. He was a business-man with a lot of business. The separation agreement provided for the applicant wife to move out of the family home and the respondent would build a bungalow for her, but he was unable to get planning permission. The husband then paid her €148,000. She was living in another town with her partner. He wanted to sell the family home and a business he owned with his brother, but could not because of the court order.

The judge said that the freezing order had arisen because of a breach in maintenance payments. Counsel for the husband said this had arisen from a mistake on the part of the bank, which it had acknowledged.

The judge said that he thought what was due to come up was a divorce and a lump sum payment in lieu of ongoing maintenance. The wife's barrister said that an application for proper provision had arisen because she had received an affidavit of means very late the previous evening, and needed time to examine it. The affidavit of means was not vouched, and she would need discovery. "In relation to a self-employed person I've always followed the practice of looking for discovery," she said. She needed an adjournment. The husband's barrister said that a purchaser was available to buy the house, but would not go ahead because of the hold-up in the family law proceedings. She asked the judge to allow the case to go ahead that day.

"If the applicant is not happy with my decision she can appeal it to the High Court," Judge Keys said, and went on: "How will that affect the sale? If a barrister says she cannot properly advise her client I have to accept it. Where does that leave us? The alternative is to put it back for a very short period of time and make such orders as allow the purchaser to proceed." The wife's barrister said that at the time of the separation the family home was valued at £72,000. It was now worth €2.9 million. That was a change in circumstances. She was happy to come to an arrangement.

There was a brief adjournment while the husband's solicitor contacted the solicitor for the purchaser of the house, and on his return he said the purchaser would go ahead if the court made an order stating the applicant wife had no interest in the family home. That was agreed, and the freezing order was lifted. The judge refused to order that the proceeds be frozen if the house was sold, apart from a sum of €75,000 and he said he would hear the case the following week.

Where substantial assets are involved, proceedings can be prolonged by discovery and other motions. Systematic case management of all family law cases could reduce this.

Case Study 7
In another case on the South-Western Circuit, this time before O'Sullivan J, a woman who had obtained a divorce in 2002 applied for a lump sum order in a "second bite" case. The couple had separated in 1988, the family home was sold and the proceeds divided, with each party getting £13,500. She entered another relationship. A consent divorce was ruled in 2002, under which no provision was sought by or made for her. She entered a third relationship, but this came to an end before these proceedings. She had not remarried. The wife said that her claim was justified by a change in her circumstances.

Counsel for the former husband said that the change in circumstances was legally in her client's favour, as he had suffered an industrial accident and lost much of the use of his right arm. He ran a small business. Counsel for the wife claimed that his accounts did not reflect the true level of his income. He had re-married since the divorce and had a child in this marriage.

He gave evidence of effectively losing contact with his former wife and children after she became involved with the other man. Then in 1996 the wife sought maintenance for the children in the District Court, which was set at £20 a week per child. No arrears in maintenance were sought. In 1999 this maintenance was increased to £40 a week. When the older child was no longer dependent the sum was increased to £50 a week for the younger child. This had always been paid, and he had since offered his daughter £100 a week as she was going to college. He had much more contact with his children from the mid-1990s and now saw them frequently. He said he had no assets he could liquidate.

Asked about the wife's consent to the terms of the divorce in 2002, her barrister said she was told by her then lawyer that she had committed fraud in relation to an application for an English divorce when she did not fulfil the residency requirement, and could go to jail. As a result she did not make an application when the case came before Moran J in 2002.

"In fairness to Judge Moran, it would have come to him as a consent," O'Sullivan J said and went on:

> "To what extent does the court go behind a consent? Do they send out their own accountants? You can't say that because he decided it in a certain way it precludes a fresh application. Judges decide all these cases on the basis of proper provision. The problem with family law cases is you are meant to ensure proper provision. It seems to me to be quite an unusual jurisdiction. Despite what parties might historically have done the judge may feel he might have to do something he would never do in a commercial case. It's a supervisory jurisdiction. If I think an intervention should be made by the court, am I prevented by the fact that Judge Moran ruled a consent? Maybe I should ask the Supreme Court."

Counsel for the husband said that a decision must be made in the light of today's circumstances, and the wife was now better off than her client, owning her own home and having an income of €30,000 a year. He was married and had another child. "He can only raise money by mortgaging his home and disadvantaging his child."

O'Sullivan J gave his decision, summarising the facts. Referring to the period between 1988 and 1996 he said:

> "There was not much emotional or other support to Mrs ... at this time. This is something I would ordinarily take into account in making proper provision. She had her own life. The reason she sought a divorce [in England] in 1992 was to try to

regularise her own position. If I was approaching this matter *de novo* I would be open to making financial adjustment orders in favour of Mrs …"

However, he recalled that no claim for financial support featured in her defence and counter-claim to the 2002 divorce application. He said he was not convinced by the evidence concerning the legal advice referring to the English divorce, as this must have been given in 2001, before the defence and counter-claim were made. "If she wished to make a claim for financial relief she should have done so and she did not."

If he was to interfere now with that consent it would have to be on the basis of something that happened since. In fact if anything her circumstances were somewhat better and her husband's somewhat worse than in 2002. Referring to a recent High Court judgment by Mr Justice Abbott he said "nothing catastrophic has happened" (*IC v MC*, unreported, January 22, 2007, High Court, Abbott J). There had to be a material change in circumstances, and there was nothing significant. He refused to make any order for maintenance under s 13 of the 1996 Act.

This was one of the very few cases where I was present in which a judgment from the superior courts was invoked by counsel for either side, and referred to by the judge.

Case Study 8
In a case on the South-Eastern Circuit before Buttimer J a wife was seeking a lump sum during judicial separation proceedings. The court was told that the couple, who had three dependent children, had separated in 2002. The wife had been paid €87,000 at that time for her share in the family home, which had been in the name of her father-in-law. The husband also had 38 acres of land worth €360,000 left to him by his father and a property in Bulgaria. His total assets were now worth over €500,000. His barrister said that the property had been inherited following the breakdown of the marriage, and the property in Bulgaria acquired with his current partner. He said the husband wanted to keep the land, which was in forestry and tillage, for his children. He also said that the applicant wife was now working full-time and did not need maintenance or a lump sum in lieu.

The wife said in evidence that she had got a county council house but could only get it if she had a waiver of her interest in the family home, so she accepted the money offered in order to get it. Her barrister put it to the husband that, with an income of over €51,000 a year, he had considerable borrowing power.

Buttimer J said that his current family home was worth €246,000, and the money paid to his wife wiped out her interest in that. This left the land, worth €360,000. She proposed he pay the wife €75,000. "This is not the equalisation of the assets, but it provides Mrs … with a nest-egg. I hope the land can be saved if possible." This was agreed by the parties, and a judicial separation was granted, with these terms made a rule of court.

Case Study 9

An appeal against a District Court order for maintenance came up before McDonagh J in Dublin Circuit Court. This was an interim matter, pending a judicial separation. The court had ordered maintenance for the wife and dependent child of €800 a month, along with the payment of the mortgage on the family home, in which she and the child were living. This was €1,900 a month, and had not been paid in recent months.

The husband's barrister said the husband could not afford to pay it. He was now living in an interest-only mortgaged apartment. She said she accepted he had an interest in various properties, but they were not producing an income at the moment. Commenting on his Affidavit of Means, the judge commented: "He eats very well." He also expressed surprise at the fact he claimed €200 a month in petrol expenses and commented:

> "He is going to have to pay the mortgage, and he is going to have to continue maintenance of €800 a month. That's €2,700. That is what I see as a reasonable interim settlement. If he needs extra cash he goes to the bank and gets a loan."

This ruling, while an interim one, illustrates the fact that judges are generally insistent that dependent children are maintained and the family home secured.

Case Study 10

In another District Court Appeal, this time in Cork before Kenny J, the mother of two children, aged 15 and 11, was seeking the committal to prison of their father for failing to pay maintenance. He had been paying €100 a week in voluntary maintenance until he lost his job following an accident in July 2005. It was agreed that it be reduced to €60 a week, but he found this impossible to pay. She then went to the District Court, which ordered a weekly payment of €150. In March 2006 he fell off a chimney and injured his knee, which required an operation. He was getting €331 a week in disability benefit. Maintenance was varied down to €40 a week. He told the court the older child was now in foster care, and the younger one lived half the week with him. He had paid €678 before Christmas, and owed €1,500.

His barrister told the court he had been a regular and prompt payer until his accident. He had already been sentenced to 16-days' imprisonment for two sums, €1,053 and €1,540. "He just can't pay these amounts at the moment," he said. "This man will get back on his feet after his operation."

The judge said he would adjourn the case until July, when he would expect the man to have saved some money and to come to court then and show he was making an effort.

FAMILY HOME

The other highly contentious issue was the family home, which often featured along with the issue of children in very contentious cases among younger couples. Among older couples, it was usually the only issue.

Case Study 1

One such case came up in Limerick before O'Donohue J where a divorce was being sought, along with a property adjustment order relating to the family home. The husband had left the family home in 1988 following a barring order. He had lived in rented accommodation since and now, aged 66, wanted to move back into the family home. He was offering his wife €60,000 for her share. He had bought it for €1,300 originally and had built an extension onto it, and it was valued at €190,000 in 2004.

The wife gave evidence of marrying in 1967 and moving into the house in 1971. The couple's four children were now grown up. She said her husband was controlling and violent, he disapproved of what the children did and that he had refused to contribute to the education of the children. "Even if your husband's a mass murderer he's entitled to something," O'Donohue J commented.

She said she had spent €60,000, borrowed from a credit union, doing up the house. The husband's barrister put it to her that she had been controlling of the children and violent towards them, which she denied.

In response to a question from the judge, she said her total assets in savings and compensation from an accident were €44,000. He asked her if she was willing to offer an amount, or if she was willing to leave it up to him. She indicated she was willing to leave it up to the judge.

Under cross-examination the man admitted he had only paid maintenance under court order, and that the wife had paid college fees for the children. He said he had €60,000 in savings. He acknowledged that the wife had spent money doing up the house. However, he insisted he had always intended to move back into the house.

O'Donohue J said he was going to give the husband a third of the net equity in the house, which he valued at €171,000 when the wife's €60,000 contribution was taken off it. He said he was allowing him to keep his savings and his pensions. With the savings and the €57,000 out of the house he should be able to get somewhere to live. He gave the wife three months to raise the money, and the property adjustment order, putting the house into her name, would then come into effect.

Here, the family home was seen in the context of the husband having moved out almost 20 years earlier, and his not having contributed significantly to the maintenance and education of the children.

Case Study 2

The value of one party's interest in the family home after moving out 20 years earlier was also examined on the South-Eastern Circuit before Buttimer J. In this case the couple had married in 1967 when the wife was aged 20 and her husband was 38. They had five children. In 1987, when the youngest child was 16, she left with another man, who was aged 22, and they went to the UK, where she obtained a divorce and married him. She was seeking a recognition of this divorce, along with half the value of the family home. She said she was entitled to it as she had worked to support the family and had reared the children.

The husband accepted that his wife had worked and reared the children until she left. He said he was now in a new relationship, and had an 11-year-old child. His barrister said that the adult children were outside the court and willing to give evidence for their father, but Buttimer J said she would not hear them. The case was adjourned for a time but no agreement was reached.

"Whether working or not, your wife raised five children and therefore contributed to the house," Buttimer J said to the husband. "No one wants to put you out of your house. To get the house into your sole name would you not accept that there is a price to be paid, in acknowledgement of her raising the five children?" She awarded the wife €25,000 for her interest in the house, with six months to pay, and recognised the English divorce.

These cases illustrate the principle that the court gives recognition to the contribution made by both parties to the marriage, either inside or outside the home, even when it was made many years before the matter comes before the court.

Case Study 3

In a case in Dublin Circuit Court there was agreement between the parties on the disposal of the family home, but the judge queried the agreement made. A couple, neither of whom was legally represented and who had one son aged 12, came to court to have a consent divorce ruled. The only asset was a family home worth about €500,000. They had agreed that the wife's interest should be bought out for €120,000, on the basis that the son would inherit the house.

McDonagh J said that this should be in writing to guarantee it, and the son's name should therefore be on the title deeds. The wife said they had considered this, but it would cost €22,000. McDonagh J said that if the order they wanted was made, there was nothing to stop the husband selling the house in a few years and moving to Spain, ignoring the agreement about the son's inheritance.

"If it was between the two of you I would not consider €120,000 to be proper provision out of a house worth €500,000," he said. "When taken into account along with your son it might be proper provision. The agreement between you about [your son's] interest should be reduced to writing." He adjourned the case until this was done.

Case Study 4

In another case on the Western Circuit the same judge had questioned an agreement where a man was seeking a divorce, unopposed by his former wife. Both were legally represented. The two children of the marriage were grown up, and the family home was worth €150,000, and had a small mortgage. He was offering his wife €33,000 for her interest in it. She was in a new relationship. She told the court she was happy with this offer. However, McDonagh J said he considered a fair distribution would be a third of the net value, and this was accepted by the parties.

This indicates that some judges inquire behind agreements to satisfy themselves that proper provision, in accordance with the constitutional imperative under Art 41 and the relevant statutory requirement, has been made for both spouses in the circumstances. However, where the couple has been legally advised other judges consider that an agreement made under legal advice constitutes proper provision.

Case Study 5

In a judicial separation case in the South-Eastern Circuit the husband sought to have the family home (worth €250,000) sold and the proceeds divided. He was a taxi-driver aged 60 and his wife, who was 62, had significant health problems and had recently been in hospital. They had eight children, seven of whom were now grown up. One child had died at the age of five. The husband was now living with a new partner in her home.

A protection order had been made against the husband in 2004, and he had been away from the family home since then. His taxi business operated in the black economy and he had tax liabilities and other debts totalling €50,000. The applicant wife was willing to take over these debts for sole ownership of the family home.

The wife said she had worked throughout the marriage as well as rearing the children. She had been very depressed by the death of her child, and had developed an alcohol problem, from which she recovered. She claimed persistent physical and verbal abuse from her husband over the years and after he left she found catalogues for headstones left behind for her to see. She made other allegations about his conduct, including his affair with the woman who was now his partner.

In evidence the husband strenuously denied the allegations of violence and made counter-claims of violence against his wife. The wife's barrister said that a daughter of the marriage was available to give evidence on conduct, but Buttimer J said she did not want to draw the children of the marriage into the case. This was a case where an adult child was being asked to give evidence, and where Buttimer J indicated (as she did in other cases I attended) that she did not consider it appropriate to draw adult children into a parental dispute.

This contrasts with the attitude taken by McMahon J (as he then was) in *R v R*, (unreported, January 18, 2005, Dublin Circuit Court) in which evidence of violence was taken from three adult children of the marriage, and this was the evidence of conduct on which the judge relied in making a finding of "gross and obvious" misconduct which he said would be unjust to disregard under s 16 of the Family Law Act 1995.

In the South-Eastern case the wife's barrister suggested that the wife had a right to residency until a divorce application, which could be made in 2008. Buttimer J accepted this suggestion, adding that one of the children might be able to help the mother raise money. The barrister for the husband said that he opposed that suggestion, to which Buttimer J replied, "I have no intention of putting [the woman] out of her home, none."

She granted a decree of judicial separation, and gave the wife the exclusive right of residency in the family home until a further order of the court. She added: "It might be useful to add I don't see it as a 50/50 split. The living circumstances of Mr and Mrs ... are vastly different."

While no final order was made in this case, the "accommodation needs" of both spouse, and how they were being met at the time, meant that the wife remained secure in her home until the divorce proceedings, while the husband remained with his new partner, even though he had no claim on her property.

Case Study 6
Another case in the South-Eastern Circuit, this time before Doyle J, concerned a house worth €95,000 on an estate where there were a number of social problems. The couple, both now on social welfare, had been married since 1973 and had separated in 2004. They had eight children, all now grown up. The wife lived in rented accommodation which was damp. She wanted her name off the family home so that she could apply for county council accommodation, and she wanted compensation for her interest in it so that she could furnish such accommodation. Her husband said he had no way to raise money, and he did not want to leave the family home because he had a number of health problems, it was close to his doctor and he was used to the area. The doctor said it would be stressful and otherwise detrimental to his health for him to move.

"This couple has been married for a long, long time," Doyle J said. She went on to say:

> "It is very sad the marriage broke down. A lot of work was done by both of them in rearing the family and keeping things on the road. Both are entitled to a share in the family home. Unfortunately it is not the case that either can buy out the other. So I am going to direct the sale of the family home. On the sale of the property and the

payment of all the bills, the net proceeds are to be divided on a 50/50 basis. If there was any way the court could have left anyone in the family home it would have done that. Unfortunately I could not. Hopefully both parties can get county council accommodation and use the money to furnish it."

This case illustrates a common dilemma for judges, where the limited resources of the family do not allow for the setting up of two independent households. In this case there were no children to house, and both parties were eligible to seek local authority housing.

Case Study 7

A case in Dublin concerned a house the husband had received on his marriage from his family as his anticipated inheritance, and which had been the family home for the duration of the marriage. The couple had met in 1980 when both were very young and they married in 1990. The house was worth €1.35 million, and had a small mortgage borrowed to renovate it, as it had previously been divided into bed-sits. He had paid the mortgage, while she paid the household bills. The couple also had an investment property, a two-bedroom flat in the same area of Dublin, worth €400,000 which also had a mortgage, paid for out of the rent. The husband sought a divorce, claiming the couple had lived separate and apart under the same roof for four years and citing *McA v McA* [2000] 2 ILRM 48, but this was disputed by the wife, who claimed they had attempted a reconciliation during that time. They had no children, as she had been unsuccessful in trying to get pregnant. He was in a new relationship and had a child in it. He was offering her €200,000 for her share in the family home, and to sign over his share of the flat to her. She wanted both properties to be sold and the proceeds divided.

He said that although the house had been an investment property for his family, he had a sentimental attachment to it. His barrister cited the *C v C* case in the High Court, where O'Higgins J had said proper provision could be made while having significant regard to the provenance of a property (unreported, July 25, 2005, High Court, O'Higgins J). While a 50/50 division was superficially attractive, the barrister said, it did not take account of the provenance of the property.

In her ruling Lindsay J said the issues were whether this was a case for divorce or judicial separation, and the property adjustment order. She said that in order to apply for a divorce the couple had to live separate and apart for four of the past five years. "I have a doubt about the marriage being over in 2001," she said. "I must on balance proceed on the basis the provisions are not complied with. So I will proceed under the 1989 Act. I have no difficulty with a judicial separation."

She said the only other real issue was the house. There was no evidence as to its value at the time of the transfer to the applicant by his family. His payment of the mortgage was set off by her contribution to the household bills. The fact that the investment property was in both names she took as evidence that everything was intended to be shared 50/50. The applicant was adamant that the family home was his, and had made an offer to the court of €350,000. This was about 25 percent of the value of the assets, which was insufficient.

Lindsay J said:

> "I have read the case law on the matter. I must decide what it fair and equitable. Everything in this relationship was fair and equal. I heard evidence of sentimental attachment. But they started their married life in that house and lived together there. The mortgage was small, but it was shared equally. I cannot see why I should do anything other than split it 50/50."

She ruled that each party had a 50 percent share in each property, and said she was giving the applicant the opportunity to buy out the respondent's share in the family home for €675,000 within six weeks.

Case Study 8

A case in Cork Circuit Court was complicated by the circumstances of the children and step-children of the couple seeking a divorce. The husband was seeking sole tenancy of the local authority house, where he had been living with the children. The wife was living with her partner in a large private house. There were four children in the family, ranging in age from 26 to 13. The third child was in a juvenile detention centre. The youngest child had been living in the family home with her father, but had had a row with him and moved in with her mother and the mother's partner. The son of this partner sometimes stayed there. The father also had a new partner, who had a 16-year-old daughter. The daughter was pregnant by the 17-year-old son of his marriage, and this young woman sometimes lived with the applicant wife. Judge Kenny said that the extra family members were not the concern of the court.

In evidence the husband said he would be homeless if he had to leave the house. His daughter had left because she did not like his rules against smoking and similar conduct. The wife said she did not pay rent to her partner, and had no security in the house. She would move back into the local authority house if she was given the tenancy of it.

"If Cupid fires his little arrow you might marry [your partner] and he could buy it?" suggested Kenny J. The wife rejected the suggestion of a pending marriage that might alter her property entitlement.

"I think Mr ... is entitled to stay on in the property but he must pay Mrs ... compensation for surrendering her interest in it," Kenny J ruled and went on:

> "I fix it at €10,000, phased over 18 months. I have no difficulty with the children moving from one house to the other but I would be concerned about those children."

Granting the decree of divorce, he ordered that the tenancy of the house be transferred into the sole name of the husband. He also made orders concerning the supervision of the youngest child.

This case illustrates the fact that the family home is not necessarily a privately-owned house. The courts can and do make orders regarding the tenancy of local authority rented accommodation.

Case Study 9

In a case on the Eastern Circuit the family home was again the main issue in a judicial separation case. It was worth €690,000 and the applicant wife was living in it with the youngest of the three children of the marriage, a boy aged 16. The husband lived in a rented cottage, and he wanted the house sold and the proceeds divided so that he could buy a home.

Granting the decree of judicial separation McCartan J said:

> "The objective is to enable people to live independently and apart with some dignity. When the main asset is the family home it should be sold to enable the parties to live separately and with dignity. The objective put forward by Mrs ... is for the house to stay undisturbed until the end of the education of the son. This is likely to be in seven years. I believe this not an unreasonable objective in normal circumstances, but not here. The house has considerable value, close to €700,000. It has three bedrooms, above and beyond the needs of her and the son. Mr ... is agreeable that she retain enough to stay in the area and for the son to continue his education and contact with his friends there. The house has the capacity to deliver an unencumbered home to Mrs ... and allow Mr ... to secure a home with a small mortgage. To say he should have nothing from it at the moment is unreasonable. I propose the family home be sold and that Mrs ... receive €400,000 and the balance go to Mr ...after the expenses of the sale."

Here the judge balanced the accommodation needs of both parties, and the educational and social needs of the dependent child, in coming up with a solution.

CONDUCT

The conduct of the parties leading up to a separation, whether leading to a judicial separation or a divorce, can be cited as relevant to proper provision (See s 20(2)(i) of the Family (Divorce) Act 1996, above, which mirrors the equivalent provision in the 1995 Act).

However, following the Supreme Court decision in *DT v CT* [2003] 1 ILRM 321 such conduct is only relevant if it is "gross and obvious", and this has meant that conduct, specifically adultery, which one of the parties may consider should be taken into account is not in fact regarded as a factor which should influence the decision of the court. In *C v C* (unreported, July 25, 2005, O'Higgins J) the High Court also gave consideration to the wife's feelings of anger and betrayal when the husband installed another woman in the family home while she and the children were on holiday, but O'Higgins J did not think it came within the parameters set by the Supreme Court. These rulings bind the Circuit Court, and Circuit Court judges rarely take account of allegations concerning conduct and, indeed, discourage the parties from raising them.

During my examination of hearings in the 2006/2007 legal year, there were three cases where the issue of conduct was pursued.

Case Study 1

In the Eastern Circuit a judicial separation case where an application for divorce was substituted was heard over three days. The parties had married in 1979 and had five children, of whom only one was now dependent. As well as the family home, the couple's assets included two other houses in Ireland and one in Spain, along with money on deposit, all of which came to €1.75 million. There was a dispute as to the liabilities, as the husband had considerable tax liabilities. It was not disputed that the assets were assembled during the marriage.

One of the liabilities, other than tax, was the cost of causing damage to land owned by the couple's adult children, which had already been the subject of a High Court case, and for which the husband was found liable. He was insisting that the assets be divided only after the deduction of the liabilities, including the costs of this case and the restitution of the land.

Initially it was indicated to the court that this would be the only issue to be determined by the court, but when the case resumed counsel for the husband said that she wanted to raise issues of conduct on the part of the wife in relation to signing cheques and alleged assaults on her client. The wife was now in the witness box. Judge McCartan said to the husband's counsel: "You opened the case on the basis that your client had no objection to a 50/50 split. Conduct is not relevant to that." She replied that she had not finished that day.

"What relevance do history and conduct have to the position put forward by your client?" the judge asked. The counsel replied "He wants to live in peace. There are extraneous issues. He was brought up on an assault charge, he was assaulted by a third party and he believes his wife was responsible for that," She continued that the husband had counter-claimed for nullity, and that psychological reports were commissioned on both parties. However, he had refused to pay for them and they were abandoned.

She said that the husband claimed that there had been difficulties in the marriage within eight months of its solemnisation. She put it to the wife that she had been under the care of a psychiatrist, that she had been abused by two of her brothers, that she had used the withholding of sex as a weapon in the marriage, that she had trapped the husband into marriage because she was pregnant. The wife responded that he was very demanding sexually when she was pregnant and that one night she told him about her brothers, and subsequently he threatened to tell everyone about her brothers and her family, at which point she broke down in the witness box.

Further cross-examination continued about disputed financial matters and about relations between the parents and the children, including allegations that the husband had beaten them. Evidence was also given by accountants about the assets and liabilities.

In giving his decision, Judge McCartan said the central issue was the division of the assets and that:

> "There was no reference made then that the sad or past history would be a factor. I am regretful that the events of today were entirely unnecessary. It is a process that has boomeranged on Mr ... There has been a washing of very private linen, which has been unfortunate."

He rejected the suggestion that the wife had any liability for the costs of dealing with the damage to the children's land, pointing out that this had not been raised in the High Court case. Turning to the question of the tax liability, he said:

> "The argument could be made that all of these assets were gained by both parties and the pluses and minuses ought to be carried between them. Given the conduct of the proceedings and the way [the husband] instructed his solicitors to conduct this case, and his conduct towards his children and in the marriage I am going to find against him."

He ordered that Mrs ... have the family home, with the mortgage paid from the money on deposit, and another property in Ireland, and that Mr ... have the remaining Irish property and the house in Spain, that an endowment policy be split, and that Mr ... retain the balance of the cash on deposit from which he could settle his liabilities. He also ordered him to pay maintenance of €300 a week for his wife and €150 a week for the dependent child. Granting the divorce, he also granted mutual barring orders.

In this case it was clear that McCartan J took two types of conduct into account: the allegations of violence by the husband against the wife and children, compounded by his conduct relating to the land owned by one of his children; and the conduct of the case itself.

Case Study 2
In a case in Cork before Kenny J one party wished to plead conduct, claiming adultery on the part of his wife, which she denied, but she acknowledged a close friendship with another man following the deterioration of her relationship with her husband. There were three young children of the marriage.

Both parties gave lengthy evidence about the gradual breakdown of the marriage. The husband hired a private investigator and taped conversations between his wife and her friend which he felt substantiated his suspicions of adultery. The wife gave evidence of him working away a lot, of her own post-natal depression and loneliness, and of their attempts to reconcile, with occasional outings to restaurants and the cinema, which did not succeed.

Kenny J indicated he was not interested in hearing about the allegations. "I think this is the first case I've gone the whole way on adultery allegations," he said. "We want to find out how best to deal with the future of the children. We've gone all around the houses on adultery and which film to go to." The husband's barrister said: "It is my client's position that a saveable marriage was killed by the adulterous behaviour."

Urging the parties to talk overnight, Kenny J said:

> "They are fortunate in having a family home worth €800,000. If it was sold, they could buy two more modest family homes. Mrs ... could be the primary carer. One of the homes could be close to the children's school. Access could be agreed. The only matter is maintenance. These are the issues in my mind. The bogey in all this is the allegation of adultery. If it was not there they might have reached agreement. I don't particularly want to hear these cases, I don't mind saying. The cross-examination has made the point there is no proof of sexual intercourse."

After discussions overnight, the case was settled.

While this case was settled, it was clear as it progressed that the judge was not interested in hearing evidence relating to the allegations of adultery, though no reference was made to the case-law of the superior courts, notably the judgment of O'Higgins J in *C and C*.

Case Study 3
Another Cork case also involved the issue of adultery, this time acknowledged by the wife. The case was a judicial separation application, heard by O'Donohue J. It had started in May 2005, and had continued intermittently over 18 days until December 2006, when it finally came to an end. There were three children of the marriage.

In evidence the wife claimed her husband was very domineering and controlling. He described his anger and hurt at her relationship, especially as the man was a close friend of his. Evidence was also given concerning the husband's income and the couple's property, and their relations with the children. The eldest, a girl, had a difficult relationship with her mother as a result of the affair.

In considering his decision, O'Donohue J said to the wife's barrister: "Address me on the conduct issue." The wife's barrister replied: "The conduct issue does arise in relation to my client. But it also arises in relation to the applicant, who was very controlling."

"The wife has to realise that the deception involved has had a major impact on his life," the judge said. "The conduct issue weighs on my mind, the husband found out about it 18 months or so into the affair. He has come across as slightly controlling. The wife has given us some idea of the background to her seeking happiness elsewhere." During these exchanges, no reference was made by counsel or the judge to the superior courts' ruling that allegations of adultery were rarely to be considered in the adjudication of family law cases.

In the course of the proceedings a share of the family home had already been awarded to the wife. O'Donohue J said he would award a figure to the wife for her maintenance, but this would not be open-ended, and would end after two years. He made it clear while hearing the evidence that the fact she was in a new relationship, where she would be pooling her resources with her new partner, was a factor in this, along with her relative youth and the fact that she was re-training to re-enter the workforce. The husband had a business and money in a bank account, and the judge ordered him to pay a lump sum to the wife to enable her to buy a house.

He urged the husband to deal maturely with the impact of the affair on the family, and to try to foster good relations between his daughter and her mother. Asked by the husband's barrister to grant the judicial separation on the grounds of adultery, he refused, stating there had been an irretrievable breakdown in the marriage. The judicial separation was eventually granted on consent, but most of the orders made had been strongly urged on the parties by the judge, who refused to grant a judicial separation on the adultery ground.

It is clear from these cases that adultery will not be considered "conduct ... such that in the opinion of the court it would in all the circumstances of the case be unjust to disregard it", unless accompanied by other types of conduct, relating to financial matters and violence. The only case of the three where conduct was taken into account in making proper provision was that in the Eastern Circuit, where McCartan J took account of three aspects of the husband's conduct: his conduct towards the children, where he had admitted administering physical punishment, and where he had damaged land belonging to some of them; his "conduct in the marriage" the details of which McCartan J did not specify; and his conduct during the proceedings, whereby he had instructed his solicitors to raise matters concerning the sexual relationship between the parties which McCartan J considered to be irrelevant and unnecessarily distressing for the wife.

FINDINGS OF THE STUDY

These cases illustrate the fact that there are both common themes and differences in emphasis among different judges and across the different circuits. They also show that cases generally fall within certain parameters. Therefore it is unrealistic for family law litigants to expect outcomes that fall outside these parameters.

Custody

In relation to children, the issue of custody is usually the first dealt with. Joint custody is the preferred option among judges, though sole custody is likely to be granted to one parent when the other has been absent from the children's lives, suffers from addiction problems, or may be a risk due to a history of violence or abuse. Joint custody does not, in itself, solve all issues, as "primary residence" or "care and control" also arises. There is a distinct preference among judges for primary care and control to go to the mother, with access to the father. There is also a preference for access to be agreed between the parents, usually in the form of alternate weekends with the father, along with a half share in school holidays and sometimes a night during the week. Where it cannot be agreed, a schedule is often worked out between the solicitors, and made a rule of court.

An order that "primary care and control" of the child or children should rest with the mother is rarely opposed by the father, and features in most consent cases where there is joint custody. In the minority of cases where the father seeks to have the children stay with him half the time, and argues for this cogently, it is most often granted. However, this does not always happen, as we have seen above.

This is likely to reflect the fact that judges favour minimising the disruption to a child's routine, especially when going to school, as evidenced by the judicial remarks to this effect above. In addition, it is true that even today, when the majority of women with children are in the work-force, they are often in part-time work or lower-paid work than their partners (see CSO and ESRI figures cited in Ch.2). Therefore they are more likely to be available to the children after school. Nonetheless, it is arguable that some of the attitudes of earlier decades, where it was felt that mothers were the natural carers especially of young children, still linger, and the importance of significant input into a child's development from both parents is an area where judicial training could usefully focus. This view, expressed in the term the "tender years" principle, is exemplified in judgments like *B v B* [1975] IR 54 and *McD v McD* [1979] ILTR, 66, though it was modified by McGuinness J in *DFO'S v CA* (unreported, April 20, 1999, High Court).

Where the mother opposes any contact between a child or children and their father she is unlikely to succeed in court, as judges uphold the principle that contact with both parents is the right of the child. However, she can frustrate contact that has been ordered by the court, giving rise to recurrent applications to the court, and, as a last resort, applications for attachment and committal. While these usually go to the District Court, which I have not examined here, I know from attending some hearings in this court that this sanction is rarely used, as a judge will be reluctant to deprive a child of his or her custodial parent. It is therefore not a very useful sanction for breach of access or custody orders, and alternative sanctions should be explored.

The issue of obtaining the views of the child or children also comes up in custody, care and control and access disputes. This can be done in two ways: through the judge talking directly to the children in his or her chambers, or via a professional assessor, normally a social worker or child psychologist. The latter is preferred by most judges, and the work of the Probation Service in this regard, which was discontinued due to lack of resources, was widely praised by judges in conversation with me. A pilot project has begun in Dublin to reinstate such reports in family law cases in the Dublin Circuit Family Court, but is not available to the District Court where it is arguably even more necessary.

When the children reach their teens some judges may consult them, though others prefer not to involve even adult children in disputes between their parents. This too is an area that would benefit from discussion among the judiciary, on the basis of looking at international jurisprudence on the issue and best practice internationally. The matter may be clarified by the courts in the future.

Overall, the courts show a willingness to review arrangements that have been made in relation to custody and access in the light of changes in circumstances as, indeed, is provided for in the statute. While it might not be desirable from the point of view of the child that his or her parents are constantly in court about their living arrangements, it will nonetheless be a comfort to a parent who feels a decision was not in the interests of the child that this decision may be reviewed in future.

Maintenance

In relation to maintenance and other financial matters, it is difficult to discern clear patterns as each case is different. However, it is clear that where there are dependent children, the earning spouse, usually the father, will be expected to pay maintenance. Even if he is unemployed, he may be expected to contribute something. Where the parent is earning the amount ranges from €50 to €150 a week, depending on income and the child's needs, though there are reported cases in the High Court where there were substantial assets and where the amount was much greater.

Maintenance for the spouse normally arises where the dependent spouse, usually the wife, has not worked outside the home for a considerable time, either because she was rearing the family or is in poor health. If she is capable of working, little or no maintenance is likely to be paid. The exception to this is where there was a history of non-payment of maintenance for the children, and she made considerable sacrifices to rear and educate them, or where the husband's payment history indicates defaulting in the future. In these cases a lump sum may be ordered to be paid to the wife in lieu of past or future maintenance.

Other Financial Issues

Where there are financial assets other than a regular income which is transparent, various issues come under consideration, including the provenance of these assets or income and the needs of each spouse. However, these issues are likely to prolong the proceedings if they are not clarified at the outset through case-management or case-progression by the County Registrar.

One surprising issue is the relative absence of pension adjustment orders, other than nominal, among the ancillary orders. A pension is often a person's second most valuable asset, after the family home. Those most likely to have a substantial pension are public sector workers and those employed by big employers. Yet it is rarely divided, and often a larger share of the family home or a lump sum is agreed or ordered, leaving the pension-holder with his or her pension intact. Sometimes orders are made for contingent benefit for the former spouse and children in the event of the pension-holder's death, but otherwise other financial orders may be made in lieu of a pension adjustment order, including a disproportionate allocation of interest in the family home.

No explanation for this was offered during the court proceedings I attended. However, it may be that the issue of pension adjustment orders is seen as overly complex by practitioners, or that litigants prefer the finality of a lump sum order or a property adjustment order relating to the family home to the ongoing link with the former spouse represented by a pension adjustment order, or that financial finality is preferred over a deferred benefit (see earlier comments).

Family Home
The family home is often the only asset held by a divorcing or separating couple, especially those of limited resources. It may be that the family home is rented from the local authority, and one party is seeking the right to sole tenancy. It may be or may have been in the process of being bought from the local authority, with a share in the net equity far from enough to allow the other party buy his or her own home. Such cases are likely to cause the court greater difficulty than cases where the resources are comfortable or ample.

It is only in the most extreme situations, where one party has deserted the family and contributed little or nothing to its welfare or to the acquisition of the family home, that some share in the family home will not be recognised by the court. We have seen in the cases described above that even when one of the parties has left the family years earlier, if he or she has made either a financial or a caring contribution, the court will grant him or her some interest in the family home. Where the parties have made an equal contribution, either through one party paying the mortgage and the other the household bills, or one party paying all expenses while the other cared for the children of the family, that share is likely to be in the region of 50/50.

In a rare written judgment on this matter, McMahon J outlined the principles he followed in relation to family assets like the family home (*R v R*, unreported, January 18, 2005, Dublin Circuit Court). He noted:

> "In normal circumstances where a breakdown occurs in such a situation, one would be disposed as a starting point to consider dividing the assets accumulated during the marriage on a more or less equal basis bearing in mind the provisions of Section

16 of the Family Law Act 1995, which obliges the court to make 'adequate and reasonable' provision for the spouses and any dependent children."

He went on to consider how a finding that the conduct of one of the spouses was "gross and obvious" might modify this principle. However, in the cases I attended the principles underlying the allocation of shares in the family home, or other assets, were rarely spelled out in detail.

An area which is likely to develop further is that of "second bite" applications, where a case has been concluded but one party returns to court seeking further financial orders on the basis of changed circumstances, as provided for in s 22 of the Family Law (Divorce) Act 1996. However, if such cases are unsuccessful, as the case described above was, practitioners may discourage clients from taking this course. As Gerry Durcan has pointed out in discussing *K v K* [2003] 1 IR 334; *WA v MA* [2005] 1 IR 1; *RG v CG* [2005] 2 IR 418; *MP v AP* (unreported, March 2, 2005, High Court, O'Higgins J) and *B v B*, (unreported, December 8, 2005, High Court, O'Higgins J) it is, as yet, difficult to discern clear judicial guidance from the superior courts on this issue (2007: 107–113).

Conduct

Another area where practitioners would be wise to discourage their clients from litigating is on the issue of conduct leading to the breakdown of the marriage. Even when adultery is involved, this is rarely likely to be taken into account by the court. The standard set by O'Higgins J in *C v C* for conduct to be taken into account in the making of ancillary orders is a high one indeed, and, however wounded a party might be by the conduct of a spouse, airing this in court will prolong the proceedings but will be unlikely to influence the outcome. Of course, if violence or, as we have seen, the conduct of the proceedings is a factor, that will be considered.

Conclusion

Overall, what emerges from this survey of a selection of cases from all eight circuits during the 2006/2007 legal year, is the fact that judges are guided by an essentially pragmatic consideration of how the parties to a marriage can proceed in the aftermath of a marriage breakdown. Rulings are forward-looking, and the history of the marriage is mainly of relevance in assisting the judge to make proper provision for the parties and dependent members of the family into the future. There is no evidence of judicial *a priori* assumptions to justify a fear that either a male or a female litigant, for example, would not receive a fair hearing. However, the capacity or otherwise of individual litigants to state their case cogently can have a bearing on the outcome of their cases. This has practical relevance where there are lay litigants.

There was little reference to the case law from the superior courts in most of the cases I attended. This could be due to a number of factors, the most likely of which is that most of these cases in the higher courts are normally based on their own facts, particularly the possession of substantial assets. This is not directly comparable to the bulk of cases heard in the Circuit Court, where the judge is often faced with the problem of making "proper provision" where the resources are simply not sufficient to support two households. There is little jurisprudence from the higher courts on this. There is also relatively little on the considerations that should apply in deciding on the custody of children, where that is disputed. As we have seen, dependent children are the most likely cause of contention in these proceedings in the Circuit Court.

In the absence of jurisprudence in these areas, it would be useful for the judiciary to find mechanisms whereby they could share their experience and their views, so that they could work towards the development of principles to guide decision-making in these areas.

Chapter 4

SOME CONCLUSIONS ON THE IRISH FAMILY LAW SYSTEM

For clarity and to set the context for my observations below, I will outline how the family law system works, insofar as it relates to judicial separation, divorce and parenting issues. I have focused on the Circuit Court, which deals with the vast majority of judicial separations and divorce, the final and legal end to a marriage. Much family law operates outside of these remedies, and intersects with them, so I will include the District Court, the first port of call for many people seeking a resolution to their family law difficulties, in my outline of how the system works.

When a couple finds that their relationship has broken down and conclude that they wish to lead separate lives, they are faced with a number of practical as well as emotional issues. If there are still dependent children, who will they live with and how will they be supported? How will both parties be supported? What will happen to the house? If the family has assets outside the family home, how will they be divided? Some couples manage to resolve these issues between themselves without involving any third party. They may be resolved informally, with one party moving away, perhaps to another country, leaving the other behind in the house rearing the children, or formally through a separation agreement.

District Court

If a person who has been separated or divorced, or who is the unmarried parent of a child, has a dispute with a former partner about custody, access or maintenance, he or she will normally process it in the District Court. If a spouse, former spouse, cohabitee or the parent of an adult abusing child is the victim of violence or the threat of violence he or she can also apply to the District Court for either a barring order or a safety order. If the application is urgent, he or she can apply for a protection order or an interim barring order without the presence of the person complained against. When a barring order or a safety order is sought, the alleged perpetrator will receive a summons and will be asked to appear in court. I have not examined such applications for this work, but they form part of the whole family law picture.

In many of the applications at which I was present the applicant and the respondent were unrepresented, at least at the initial stage. However, some of the applicants to the District Court are in receipt of social welfare or on low earnings, and are eligible for legal aid, though they may have to wait some weeks to get it. According to the 2006 Legal Aid Board Annual Report, law centre solicitors represented clients in 836 custody and access disputes, 768 maintenance disputes, 633 child-care matters, 535 domestic violence matters and 336 other family law matters, all under the jurisdiction of the District Court, a total of 3,108 in 2006 (Legal Aid Board, *Annual Report 2006*: 16). However, there were 20,900 family-law applications to the District Court that year (Courts Service Annual Report 2006: 127), suggesting those in receipt of legal aid in District Court applications represented about 15 percent of the total, although some applicants are privately represented, and even allowing for the fact that many of these applications may be repeat applications, or multiple applications arising out of the same dispute, a high proportion of those appearing before the District Courts represent themselves. They often need the assistance of court staff in filling in forms, though the staff cannot offer legal advice.

In matters relating to children, the court can ask for Section 20 reports from the HSE on the situation of the child, to assist the court in making a decision on the child's welfare. This is likely to happen where there is a dispute about custody or access involving serious allegations against one or other parent. However, there is a waiting period for such reports, and this can delay the court in coming to a decision.

Decisions made in the District Court can have far-reaching implications for families, as they can decide who children are to live with, who pays to maintain them and how much, and whether a partner can live in the family home if he or she has been accused of violence or abuse. Orders made in the District Court can become "facts on the ground" when later applications are made to the Circuit Court for judicial separation or divorce, and this court may confirm the District Court orders without any further discussion. As we seen above, often the parties confronting such life-changing issues are unrepresented at what are frequently brief hearings.

Appeal to Circuit Court

This raises very serious issues for both for the administration of justice and for family law jurisprudence. If one of the parties is dissatisfied with the outcome of proceedings, he or she can appeal to the Circuit Court, where the case is reheard. However, an unrepresented litigant may find it difficult to argue his or her case adequately on appeal. If he or she loses in the Circuit Court, there is no further appeal possible, though issues relating to custody of and access to children can go back to the Court on the grounds that circumstances have changed.

Judicial Review in the High Court

If a case is heard in a perfunctory manner in the District Court, or if mistakes are made by the presiding judge, it is open to one or other of the parties to seek a judicial review in the High Court. However, an unrepresented litigant would be unlikely to know this, and would be highly unlikely to be capable of taking a judicial review even if he or she did know it was possible. The Legal Aid Board, whose resources are limited, is reluctant to spend those resources taking judicial reviews. Therefore the type of decisions that are made in the District Court in family law are very rarely examined in the superior courts, meaning that these issues of fundamental importance to individual families and to society receive scant scrutiny from the courts, and produce very little jurisprudence. This is a very serious matter from the point of view of the development of family law jurisprudence. Contrast this with, for example, road traffic offences like drink driving which, because of the financial and legal resources available to some of those charged with such offences, have been frequently and exhaustively examined by the superior courts.

Judicial Separation and Divorce

The District Courts cannot, of course, grant judicial separations or divorces, though they can deal with issues that are often related, like child-related matters and maintenance. The Circuit Court and the High Court enjoy concurrent jurisdiction in relation to judicial separation and divorce, though the overwhelming majority of cases (98.4 percent in 2006) are heard in the Circuit Court.

If the parties are married and have lived apart informally for a number of years, once that period has reached or exceeded four years the situation can be formalised through applying for a divorce and any orders relating to property and children issues as have been agreed. If there are no matters in dispute, this can be done by seeking the appropriate forms from one of the parties' local Circuit Court office, filling them in and bringing an application for a divorce to the Circuit Court. It will be necessary to make a number of attempts to contact the other party in order to inform him or her of the application and seek his or her input into the proceedings. However, if these attempts fail, the applicant spouse can go ahead with the application and a divorce can be granted on an uncontested basis (provided the court is satisfied that the couple have been apart for four years, there is no reasonable prospect of a reconciliation, and proper provision, in the circumstances, has been made for the parties and other dependent members of the family).

"DIY Divorces"

Where a divorce is uncontested, and an individual does not see the need for legal assistance but feels unable to process the form-filling him or herself, he or she may seek the help of one of the "DIY Divorce" businesses that exist around the country. These are run by non-lawyers who will talk a person through the formalities necessary to obtain an uncontested divorce, and help them acquire the necessary documentation (normally the marriage certificate) and fill in the forms. Some concerns have been expressed by practitioners in conversation with me about divorce applications coming through such agencies, but it is beyond the scope of this work to examine them. Clearly practitioners have a vested interest in not losing clients to such agencies, but from a client's point of view they can offer a financially attractive alternative to legal assistance.

Mediation

Where the couple is in dispute about the break-up of the relationship and the arrangements for the future, one option available to resolve these issues is mediation. This involves the couple seeking the services of a trained mediator who will help them define what they want and facilitate them in coming to a mediated agreement. That can then become a civil agreement or can be made binding through being brought before a court. The mediator may work for the State Family Mediation Service or be an independent practitioner. Mediators with the Family Mediation Service must be registered with the Mediators Institute of Ireland, but there is nothing to stop anyone calling themselves a family mediator and setting up in private practice, as the profession is unregulated. Some mediators have a legal background, some do not (for a full discussion of both the theoretical and practical aspects of the use of mediation in Ireland, see Sinead Conneely, *Family Mediation in Ireland* 2002). Proposals for the future use of mediation and other forms of alternative dispute resolution are contained in the Law Reform Commission's recently-published and exceptionally thorough *Consultation Paper on Alternative Dispute Resolution,* (LRC CP 50-2008).

For a couple who remains unaware of how mediation may help them, or does not see mediation as an option, or who tries it without reaching a settlement, the next step is to seek legal assistance, either to negotiate a separation or to pursue the disputed issues through the courts. For people of limited means, this can be done through the Legal Aid Board.

Legal Aid

Eligibility for aid through the Legal Aid Board is quite restricted. Only those with a disposable income of less than €18,000 qualify (Legal Aid Board Information Leaflet No 13). While disposable income is calculated after specified allowances are given for a dependent spouse, children, child-care costs, accommodation, income tax and PRSI, an earning applicant with a dependent spouse and two children, earning just above the average industrial wage of €31,000, would barely qualify if there was no other income into the house. Ironically, the dependent spouse, if he or she had only a part-time income or social welfare payments, probably would qualify for legal aid, and would reduce the deductions the earning spouse could claim. If the earning spouse was unable to afford a private solicitor (as would be very likely for a person on or just above the average industrial wage) this would lead to an inequality of arms before the court. This is an issue that requires closer attention from legislators and policy-makers.

If a person does not qualify for legal aid, he or she must either seek the assistance of a private solicitor or attempt to represent him or herself. If the issue goes to court, a barrister will normally also be retained by the solicitor (a personal litigant cannot brief a barrister). This method of resolving family disputes can be very costly indeed if court proceedings are involved.

Collaborative Law

Recently a method of resolving family disputes without going to court, while protecting the legal rights of both parties, has been developed by some family law solicitors in Ireland. Called collaborative law, it involves both parties, along with their solicitors, agreeing to enter a process where they will all seek the best outcome for all concerned, especially the children. If and when this leads to a settlement, the settlement is brought to court and made a rule of court, and thereby is legally binding. However, it only works if both parties are wholeheartedly committed to an amicable and forward-looking solution to the breakdown of their relationship. If the collaborative effort breaks down the parties must engage new solicitors and start on the contested process from scratch, as the traditional methods of the adversarial system, where no weakness is revealed to the other side, will have been given up in the collaborative process.

Family Law Proceedings—The Procedure

Once a person embarks on family law proceedings, a Family Law Civil Bill is issued. The contents of the Civil Bill and necessary procedures were drawn up by the court Rules Committee, and the Bill will outline the basis for the action and the reliefs being sought by the person making the application. It may include pleadings, that is, the arguments on which the application for a judicial separation or divorce is grounded. The reliefs sought will normally relate to property, maintenance and children, as well as a decree of judicial separation or divorce. Where financial reliefs are being sought, it will also be accompanied by an Affidavit of Means (setting out the person's income and expenditure) and, if there are children, an Affidavit of Welfare, outlining where they live, any special requirements, how they are being cared for and whether this is likely to change. The Civil Bill will be sent to the other party, who will have a period of time in which to respond with a defence and counter-claim. The other party will be warned that failure to respond can be taken, ultimately, as consent, so sometimes the divorce is proceeded with without the other party, particularly if the other party is living abroad and cannot be contacted.

The language in which the Family Law Civil Bill is couched is very adversarial, and can include an extensive exposition of the reasons why the applicant finds it unreasonable to live with the respondent, and a very long list of proposed reliefs, including sole custody of dependent children, highly restricted access to them for the other parent, sole occupancy of the family home and its transfer into the name of the applicant, maintenance for both the children and the applicant spouse, a pension adjustment order, other financial orders including a lump sum, and, if there has been any suggestion of domestic violence, barring or safety orders. Often most of these reliefs do not ultimately form part of an agreed settlement or are not granted by the court when it makes its final orders. They mirror the type of claims made in other actions, like personal injury actions. However, the very fact that they are sought as part of the opening salvos in the family law action is not conducive to an amicable outcome, and runs counter to the necessity for the parties to maintain cordial relations if they continue to parent dependent children. It is, of course, an argument that points not made in the initial pleadings cannot later be raised in further proceedings, but the manner in which family law proceedings are conducted should receive more close and sensitive attention from the practitioners' professional bodies.

The other party is likely to contest some or all of the pleadings made by the initiating party, especially if he or she does not agree to the reliefs being sought, and wishes to put forward other solutions to the issues at stake. A Defence is then filed. If the respondent party does not wish to proceed quickly to resolve the issues, he or she can seek an adjournment in order to prepare a Defence. This process can be dragged on for a considerable time.

At this stage other issues may arise, for example, disputes about the financial affairs of either or both parties. This can lead to motions for Discovery, where the County Registrar or the Court can order that documentary evidence be produced concerning the earnings, assets and liabilities of the parties. Even after Discovery, there may be disputes about the completeness of the documentation produced, and professionals like forensic accountants may be engaged. There may also be disputes about the value of property, requiring evidence from valuers.

Alternatively, or in addition, there may be a dispute concerning the welfare and future of the children. Section 47 of the 1995 Family Law Act empowers the Circuit or High Court to order a social report relating to a party to the proceedings, or any other person to whom the proceedings relate, including children. The court may also order an investigation into the welfare of the child under s 20 of the Child Care Act 1991. Thus, one or other party may ask the court for an independent report on the children, usually carried out by the HSE or a psychologist or psychiatrist who interviews the children and the parents, writes a report and is prepared to give evidence to the court on it. Obtaining such a report may take many months, and can cause further delays and expense.

Eventually, in such a contested case, the application for judicial separation or divorce will get to court. In many instances this will be the first time since the process began that the parties and their legal representatives are in the same building. This provides an opportunity for a discussion of the issues, and negotiations often take place in the vicinity of the court on the day the case is due to proceed. During the "call-over", when the listed cases are called out and the parties or their legal representatives tell the judge whether they are ready for the case to proceed, it is not uncommon for them to tell the court that talks are going on, but ask for the case to be left in the list in case the talks do not succeed. Even when a case begins, and evidence is heard, talks can go on during lunch-time or at the end of a day's hearing, which can lead to an announcement when it is due to resume that it has been settled. Some judges suggest an adjournment during the case for the purpose of allowing discussions to take place. It is clear that an opportunity for negotiations often occurs very late in what is already an adversarial process, and it is equally clear that a process that required earlier negotiations could benefit all the parties concerned. The fact that 91 percent of cases are eventually settled underlines the fact that negotiations should be embarked upon as soon as possible in order to avoid unnecessary conflict and expense.

The Hearing

If a trial is fully heard, the applicant first gives evidence, starting with the date of the marriage and the names and ages of the children, if any. Prompted by his or her counsel, he or she explains when and how the marriage broke down, outlining the background to the breakdown if this is one of the issues in contention between the parties, and how he or she now wishes to see all the issues resolved. For example, the applicant may, at this stage, explain to the judge why he or she thinks that they should be allowed live in the family home, have custody of the children, and receive a substantial amount of money to maintain themselves and the children. The barrister for the other party, the respondent, will cross-examine the applicant on those parts of his or her evidence that are in dispute. The barrister will then call his or her own client, who will give their side of the argument, and outline what they want as an outcome to the case. The applicant's barrister may cross-examine the respondent.

Further evidence may be called, normally in relation to property matters or issues relating to children. Such evidence could be either in documentary form, or expert witnesses may be called. When all the evidence has been heard the judge will give his or her decision. Normally the judicial separation or divorce is granted if the conditions concerning the length of the separation or the other grounds outlined in the legislation have been met. This is usually accompanied by the extinction of the parties' mutual succession rights, though occasionally, if the judge feels that one party has not been adequately provided for during the marriage, or will not be following its dissolution, the succession rights of that party may be preserved. The judge will also grant what are known as ancillary orders, relating to the family home, children, maintenance and other property issues. If there has been a history of family violence, barring orders may be included with the ancillary orders.

Applications for Custody and Maintenance

Matters relating to custody of and access to children, and to the maintenance of spouses and children, can be brought to court independently of applications for separation or divorce. Both the District and the Circuit Courts have jurisdiction to hear such applications. Usually if a case is already before the Circuit Court as a divorce or judicial separation application, and interim custody or access or maintenance are required, this is dealt with by that court. If a divorce or a judicial separation has been granted, matters relating to maintenance, custody and access can be referred to the District Court.

Decisions of the District Court on these issues, or on domestic violence orders, can be appealed to the Circuit Court. Decisions of the Circuit Court on all family law matters (other than District Court appeals) can be appealed to the High Court, which will then hear the case, or that portion of it that relates to the matter under appeal, afresh. Obviously, preparing a case for a Circuit Court hearing where there is a full dispute and expert witnesses, followed by an appeal to the High Court with the same evidence, depending on the extent of the dispute, will be very costly.

Both the High Court and the Circuit Court also have jurisdiction to hear applications for nullity. This is relatively rare, with 25 granted in the Circuit Court in 2006, and none in the High Court (Courts Service *Annual Report* 2006: 124), and it did not form a major part of the project, so I do not consider it necessary to describe this procedure.

FLAWS IN THE SYSTEM

There are various points where inefficiencies and anomalies in the family law system can be identified, and where opportunities for exacerbating the conflict can be seen.

In practice the District Court hears the bulk of cases involving guardianship, maintenance, custody and access where the parents are unmarried, as well as hearing applications referred to it from the Circuit Court when it has already dealt with judicial separation and divorce. It is often the first port of call for a person in a family dispute situation. While this study did not examine District Court hearings, some points can be made about family law in this jurisdiction from the available statistics.

Given the volume of family law involved, it is a tribute to the judges and staff in the District Court that they manage to deal with it at all. In 2006 the District Court heard 5,027 applications for custody and/or access, 1,742 applications from non-marital fathers for guardianship, 2,652 applications for maintenance from unmarried parents, and 1,493 applications for maintenance from married parents. Almost 10,000 (9,924) applications were made under the Domestic Violence Act 1996, bringing the total number of family law applications to 20,900 (Courts Service *Annual Report 2006*: 127).

This is an enormous volume of work, carried out with little or no ancillary resources or support, and where outside of Dublin there is no dedicated Family District Court. In addition, there are a growing number of non-Irish nationals using the District Court in family law matters (anecdotal evidence from District Court judges). This puts an added strain on resources because they sometimes need interpreters, and usually require legal representation, as they have little understanding of the Irish legal system. For all these reasons, family law applications to the District Court are frequently rushed, and parties may not have the time to outline adequately their case and concerns.

In order to improve the service to those involved in family law disputes, which are especially traumatic for all concerned and impact on vulnerable children and adults, consideration should be given to providing special support to family law at District Court level. This should include allocating judges with a special interest in, and experience of, family law to hear family law cases outside Dublin (in Dublin judges are already allocated to Dolphin House exclusively for a period).

Inevitably, cases have to be disposed of quickly. The sheer pressure of numbers of litigants may have an inhibiting effect on the amount of evidence that is heard, compounded by the fact that most litigants are not legally represented (see figures above for Legal Aid Board representation). This can lead to some litigants or respondents not being adequately heard. There is no possibility of a written decision. Reasons may not be given verbally for the decision made. The only record that exists is the order recorded by the court clerk.

ECHR Concerns

All this is very unsatisfactory from a number of points of view, and may well place Ireland in breach of Art 6 of the European Convention on Human Rights (ECHR), which guarantees the right to a fair trial. A person seeking adjudication of his or her dispute could leave the court with a decision they do not understand, and for which no reasons were given. While every person whose case is decided by the District Court has the right to appeal to the Circuit Court, such an appeal must effectively be a re-hearing of the action, as no record of the original trial exists. Indeed, this is also the case with Circuit Court cases, as no transcript exists of them either, and each High Court appeal is therefore a re-hearing of the case.

If a disappointed litigant seeks a judicial review of the court's decision, challenging the way it was arrived at, the High Court has nothing to rely on but the claims of the litigant, which may or may not be supported by his or her legal representative, if there was one. This is very unsatisfactory both from the point of view of the litigant and that of the judge in the original trial. In fact there are very few judicial reviews of family law cases. This is not necessarily because no issues arise concerning how they are processed in the District Court, but is more likely because those involved are unrepresented, or represented by the under-resourced Legal Aid Board, so decisions of this Court in the family law area are rarely examined by the superior courts.

Many of the issues concerning the recording of decisions and the reasons for them can be dealt with in the future through digital recording, which is at present being piloted by the Courts Service in certain courts, and procedures for accessing transcriptions of these recordings by the litigants and by those involved in any appeal proceedings can then be developed.

Alternative Dispute Resolution

Sections 5 and 6 of the Judicial Separation Reform Act 1989 and ss 6 and 7 of the Family Law (Divorce) Act 1996 require that a solicitor draws a client's attention to the options of counselling and mediation, and must provide a certificate saying that he or she has discussed this option with the client before the practitioner processes the case through the courts. However, in practice this legislation appears to have little bearing on the use of mediation by those whose relationships have broken down and in conversation with me some judges expressed scepticism as to whether the option of mediation is seriously discussed by many solicitors with their clients.

Mediation

In 2006 1,494 couples sought the assistance of the Family Mediation Service (the "FMS"), of whom 875 participated in the mediation process. Of these, 488 (56 percent) reached agreement, 51 (six percent) returned to their marriages, and 319 (38 percent) did not complete the mediation process (Family Support Agency *Annual Report 2006*: 25). However, according to an interview with Mary Lloyd of the FMS, many of these couples said that the mediation process, though ultimately unsuccessful, helped them to clarify the issues they needed to resolve in another way.

Mediation can be used in coming to an agreement about legal separation or divorce. An agreement on divorce can also be finalised in the Circuit Court (or High Court in a small number of cases), and the terms of a separation agreement can subsequently be imported into a consent divorce, and made a rule of court. Mediation is also sometimes used in cases involving custody of and access to children, and maintenance, matters which mainly go to the District Court. However, the FMS does not have a breakdown of the issues that the couples using its service sought to have resolved. It is likely that the FMS clients would otherwise have ended up in either the Circuit or the District Court. Therefore the 875 couples (1,750 individuals) who sought its services in 2006 need to be seen in the context of the 20,900 family law applications to the District Court, the 5,835 applications to the Circuit Court and the 90 to the High Court (all these figures exclude s 33 applications, seeking permission under s 33 of the Family Law Act 1995 to marry without the statutory notice), which come to a total of 26,825 court applications in the area of family law that year. Each application represents a couple, as each case has an applicant and a respondent. In addition, thousands of couples negotiate a solution to their dispute outside court, usually with the assistance of lawyers.

Even accepting that a number of these applications, especially in the District Court, relate to the same family dispute, it shows the number who use the FMS to be a drop in the ocean, about three percent of the total seeking a resolution of their family disputes. While there are no figures available for the use in family law of private mediators who might be used in coming to separation agreements or in formulating the consent terms in the divorce, it is unlikely they would make a significant dent in the overall figures, especially as separation agreements negotiated outside court proceedings are not included in the total number of court applications.

The limited use of mediation can be for a number of reasons. In Ireland, unlike in many other common law jurisdictions, there is no obligation on a couple to undergo any mediation before having recourse to the courts (see Conneely, 2002 for an examination of the use of mediation in other jurisdictions). Some legal practitioners have concerns about the quality of mediation available in certain areas, and fear that their client's rights may not be upheld during the process, especially where there is an imbalance in power and resources between the parties. It is also a fact that a client opting for mediation is a client lost to a solicitor, which may have a bearing on the extent to which solicitors encourage their clients to seek a mediated settlement.

Unpublished research carried out by researchers linked to the FMS also found that both the public and the legal professions lacked information about the service and what it can do, which contributes to it not being used more (as discussed in an interview between the author and Mary Lloyd, FMS). Yet it is used to the fullest extent of its capacity, as it only has four full-time offices and 12 part-time offices, open, at most, a few days a week. This writer was told that the FMS was unable to take up offers of rooms in Phoenix House and Dolphin House in Dublin, where the Circuit and District Courts hear family law, due to lack of resources. If there was a greater demand for the service there would be a stronger case for greater resources. Lack of information, lack of enthusiasm about mediation among solicitors, and lack of resources in the service all feed off each other to keep the numbers using this service small.

It was clearly the intention of the legislature that mediation should play a role in the resolution of family disputes (ss 6 and 7 of the Family Law (Divorce) Act 1996) and it is obvious that this area of law is particularly unsuited to the adversarial legal system. Certain issues in family law, notably those to do with the welfare of children, require ongoing cooperation between the parents where at all possible. Once a dispute about children reaches the courts, with allegations and counter-allegations flying and, sometimes, the assistance of experts invoked on both sides, damage to the children and to their relationship with their parents becomes very difficult to avoid. Furthermore, a solution imposed by a judge is likely to leave one or other party dissatisfied and reluctant to make it work, fuelling further ongoing conflict.

For these reasons, in many jurisdictions mediation sessions on child-related matters are mandatory, and cases cannot reach the courts without at least an attempt at mediation. Scotland provides a good example of the use of mediation in child-related disputes. The term mediation covers a wide range of different practices, including both court-ordered and voluntary mediation, and it is outside the scope of this work to examine the discipline in detail. This has been done by Sinead Conneely who has pointed out that it is an area where empirical research is difficult, given the wide range of different practices (2002: 87). However, she points out that:

> "substantial evidence testifies to high rates of user satisfaction across all forms of family mediation and across jurisdictions… Mediation also seems to be associated with higher rates of compliance than adjudication, with high rates of settlement and compromise and it may be more appealing to the divorcing population in terms of cost, although the jury is still out on that question." (2002: 159).

The issue of alternative dispute resolution in all civil law, including family law, is dealt with by the Law Reform Commission in its 2008 Consultation Paper on the issue (LRC, 2008). There were submissions made to this paper up to the end of October 2008, with a report to then be written and published, so change in the use of alternative dispute resolution may follow.

The topic of this work, however, is what happens when cases come to court, and it is to this study that we now return.

FINDINGS OF THE STUDY

The study reported in Ch.2 and Ch.3 allow certain tentative conclusions to be drawn. The first of these is that about 91 percent of all judicial separation and divorce cases settle. However, this figure disguises the fact that some settlements come after the litigation process has started, and there may be multiple interim applications and motions for discovery, along with a part-hearing of the case, before a case settles. The costs of settling such a case will be considerable. On the other hand, there are numerous divorce cases in particular where no orders are made other than those extinguishing the parties' succession rights, and where little or no costs are incurred. Given that most cases eventually settle, methods should be explored to structure the means by which a settlement can be achieved early in the process of separation or divorce.

Gender

The study also shows that female applicants outnumber men by about 58 percent to 42. However, there is a much greater divergence when it comes to judicial separations, and the proportions are more equal among divorce applicants.

As stated above, this probably reflects the greater number of reliefs sought by applicants for judicial separation as opposed to divorce, where often the only reliefs sought are the decree and confirmation of terms already reached or ordered at separation stage. This is likely to reflect the higher level of dependency among women (see CSO figures quoted above), and their consequent urgent need for a resolution of financial matters. Judicial separations were also more contentious than divorces, with 40 percent of the cases which were fully contested in Ch.3 being judicial separations, compared with only 11 percent of divorces.

Age of Applicants
The study shows that both judicial separations and divorces are sought by couples in all age-groups, and therefore by people with a wide spectrum of needs, relating to the stage of life they have reached. Policy-makers and legislators cannot act on the basis that there is a typical applicant, or typical respondent, in a family law case, and should be wary of responding only to the demands of a vociferous sub-group among family law litigants.

Custody and Access
Issues to do with children emerged as the most contentious issue, with 73 of all contested cases referred to in Ch.3 concerning children. Yet it should be noted that the issue of dependent children only arises in a minority (37 percent) of all family law cases. Maintenance (often in tandem with children) and the family home were the other contentious issues. Yet there is little jurisprudence on the principles that should inform decisions concerning the custody of and access to children, and jurisprudence concerning maintenance and the family home tends to derive from asset-rich cases. This poses questions for the judiciary, in terms of finding ways to share its views and experience; and for practitioners, in terms of tempering the expectations of their clients with realism.

What this study shows is that the courts do operate within certain parameters, even though there is variation within them. Following the breakdown of a marriage, dependent children end up living mainly with their mother in almost 60 percent of cases. This can either be because the mother has sole custody or, in the majority of cases, because there is joint custody but with "primary care and control" resting with the mother. When the issue of custody is contested and this latter arrangement is the outcome, there is, as we saw in Ch.3, little reasoning offered to justify it. However, as we have also seen, if the mother has addiction problems or has effectively abandoned the family, she is unlikely to have custody of the children, and if the father argues cogently for half the care and control he is quite likely to get it.

It is clear from the data compiled by the CSO and the ESRI that these outcomes usually represent a continuation of the care-sharing prior to the couple separating. However, it may not necessarily correspond to the best interests and emotional needs of both children and adults post-separation. There is clearly a need for research that challenges the assumptions that may underly this default position, and for further education among the judiciary to ensure that the outcomes of disputes about custody are evidence-based and correspond to the best available practice.

Family Home

The family home is, as we have seen, sold in only a minority of cases. In most cases one or other party is given possession of it, normally on the payment of a sum to the other party, or instead of past or future maintenance, or on taking over the payment of the mortgage, if there is little equity in the family home, or a combination of some or all of these. The facts of each case determine the outcome here, but different weight is given to different factors by different judges. In particular, the presence of young children, and their attachment to their home, is likely to be given weight. Here, again, it would be helpful for litigants and practitioners to know what factors would be brought to bear in a decision.

Maintenance

Maintenance and other financial matters are decided according to the terms of the Family Law (Divorce) Act 1996 and the Family Law Act 1995. However, the list of considerations that the court has to take into account is long, and the legislature gave no indication as to the relative weight to be accorded to different items on it. Each judge therefore must exercise his or her own discretion in allocating priorities to the different elements in the legislation, and there is little guidance from the higher courts on what those priorities might be.

From the cases described in Ch.3, however, it is possible to conclude that an earning spouse (normally the husband/father) will be expected to pay maintenance for dependent children, even if they live part of the time with him. There appears to be a widespread assumption among the judiciary that the husband/father is the main earner in most families, an assumption borne out by the CSO statistics quoted in Ch.2 above. Even where the mother is working, it is rare (though not unknown) that she is asked to pay maintenance, even when the children live most of the time with their father. When children are no longer dependent, however, and the only dependent is the spouse, maintenance is the exception rather than the rule. If the wife has worked in the home rearing the family, sometimes (as we have seen from the cases described) supplementing the family income with part-time work, this will be reflected in her receiving a larger share of the family home when it comes to be divided, rather than ongoing maintenance, though that is sometimes paid.

Conduct

As has already been stated, conduct is unlikely to be a factor in the eventual outcome of a case, unless it meets a very high threshold in terms of being "gross and obvious". Factors which might contribute to this would include persistent violence, and the conduct of a case in a way that increased the stress on the other party and wasted the time of the court.

It should be possible, therefore, for both mediators and legal practitioners to outline to their clients the broad parameters within which either a settlement or a court decision will come. Practitioners in particular should avoid encouraging unrealistic expectations among their clients. In addition, the difference between what is obtainable through negotiation and what is available in court is unlikely to be very great in most cases; therefore the perils and cost of going to court should be made known to litigants before they embark on this path.

SUGGESTIONS FOR CHANGE

Legislation

The constitutional and statutory framework of our family law system drives people inexorably into a two-stage process. As a divorce cannot be obtained until the parties have lived separate and apart for four out of the previous five years, when a marriage breaks down there are many matters requiring urgent resolution which cannot wait for four years. The parties need to resolve matters like where each of them, and the children, if there are any, will live; what access arrangements there will be for the non-custodial parent; what will become of the family home; and what financial arrangements will be put in place to secure the day-to-day living expenses of the parties and their children. These are often resolved through a separation agreement or a judicial separation.

When the parties seek a divorce four years later, the terms of this agreement, or judicial separation, can be re-opened as the judge is obliged to be satisfied that "proper provision" has been made for both spouses, any dependents of the family and any other person prescribed by law. This means that two sets of proceedings are often needed. The legal solution of a judicial separation, designed for circumstances where divorce was not legal in Ireland and widely expected to fade away when divorce was introduced, has become an integral part of the legal armoury of family lawyers, adding to stress and expense for litigants.

The Constitution stipulates that no court can grant a divorce until the parties have lived apart for at least four years, and that it is satisfied that proper provision has been made for the spouses, children and any other person prescribed by law, and this can only be changed by constitutional referendum. However, the legislation governing divorce could be amended to permit a divorce to be sought, and to grant certain ancillary reliefs, with the proviso that the final decree of divorce could only be granted after four years, without a requirement for a constitutional referendum. While the process would still involve two stages, it would more closely resemble the British system of two decrees, a decree nisi and a decree absolute, save with the difference that here the ancillary reliefs would come first. Such an approach would find support in the jurisprudence set by *T and T*, where the Supreme Court stated that certainty was desirable.

The In Camera *Rule*

The new regime concerning the *in camera* rule has permitted limited reporting of family law, which has been continued by the Courts Service. However, while individual academic researchers have been present to examine specific aspects of family law in court, no other organisation has been carrying reports, and it is uncertain how long the Courts Service project will continue. This means that accurate and informed reporting on family law is not guaranteed to find its way into the mainstream media and into public discourse.

One of the outcomes of the project has been to prove that family law cases can be reported without identifying the parties. This should reassure those concerned about allowing the media to report on such proceedings. The Regulations should now be amended to permit media reporting, subject to conditions similar to those laid down in the Protocol governing the Courts Service project. This would subject the family courts to the same scrutiny as applies to all other courts and assure the public that justice was being done, while protecting the anonymity of the parties, as required by the legislation.

Alternative Dispute Resolution

If a consensus exists that the adversarial legal system is not suited to family law, measures should be taken to reduce the use of this system to a minimum. This should start with directing people toward alternative dispute resolution, then designing pleading and defences in a manner least likely to inflame the situation, and ensuring cases are managed in such a way as to isolate the issues in dispute and minimise the matters tried in court, along with motions and interim applications.

There are different ways in which alternative dispute resolution should be made the first port of call for those involved in family law disputes. Measures could be undertaken to oblige the parties in family law disputes to attempt mediation before having recourse to the courts, especially where children are involved. This would require legislative change, an expansion of the FMS and a national system of accreditation for mediators. In the meantime, a concerted and coordinated effort could be made by the FMS and the Courts Service to outline all the methods available to deal with family disputes, including mediation.

It should also be possible for judges, through a Practice Direction, to insist on a minimum number of mediation sessions taking place before a case could be placed on the list for hearing. Alternatively, there could be a standard preliminary hearing where the court could establish whether a case could be remitted to mediation, coupled with an order for disclosure of assets where this was an issue. The court could also take the opportunity to indicate to the litigants that unreasonable expectations would not be entertained.

Even if mediation fails, it should be possible through it to isolate what the difficult issues are, or whether one of the parties has felt disadvantaged by the process. Such a case may be suitable for seeking the assistance of collaborative law. This is in use both by private practitioners and by those working with the Legal Aid Board. Mediators should inform the parties about how the outstanding issues could be resolved through collaborative law, and be able to inform them about available practitioners. There are ways in which collaborative law can be combined with mediation. If clients first seek the services of collaborative lawyers, and meet an obstacle in their discussions, this could be resolved through mediation.

Not every family dispute is suitable for either mediation or collaborative law. Further, every citizen is entitled to access to the courts to seek their assistance in resolving disputes. Inevitably, some family law issues will end up before the courts for adjudication. However, everything possible should be done to ensure that when this happens the case is as non-contentious as the practitioners and the judge can make it, and that it progresses as quickly and smoothly as possible. That does not happen at the moment.

Family Law Civil Bill
At the outset, some attention should be given to the form taken by the Family Law Civil Bill. Without compromising the rights of those who seek the assistance of the courts, the parties to a family law action should not be seen by the legal system as adversaries. Unlike most other litigants, if they have children, including adult children, they are likely to need to continue some form of relationship into the future as they relate to the children, grandchildren and the extended family. The welfare of other people, especially children, could depend on the nature of that relationship. While ensuring that the citizen's right to due process is upheld, the language in which his or her entitlement to reliefs is couched, and the desirability of alternatives to litigation in family law matters, should be considered by the Rules Committee in drafting a new form of Family Law Civil Bill.

Delay
Delays in cases coming to court are endemic at Circuit Court level, though a distinction must be drawn between the Circuit Family Court in Dublin and the Circuit Courts hearing family law outside Dublin. Generally three courts sit in Dublin in a dedicated court on a full-time basis. As a result there is no serious problem of delays arising from lack of court time. If a case is adjourned a date can usually be set within a relatively short time. There is no necessity for the judges to sit long days. None of these apply to the courts outside Dublin.

This is not to say that the system in Dublin could not be improved. All cases are listed for 10.30am, though in reality many have no hope of being heard until the afternoon. Consent cases are listed on the same day as cases due to be heard, so that cases only requiring a few moments of the court's time in order to be ruled can be waiting for a considerable time. This means that litigants and their representatives are crowded together in the waiting area for hours at a time.

Outside Dublin there are consistent complaints of delays, arising from too few family law days in many circuits. According to some practitioners and court staff, in places where delays are very long people can end up settling on terms they are unhappy with, just to bring an end to the proceedings. In counties outside Dublin and Cork there are only one or two weeks of family law a term, consisting of, at most, four days. As a result the lists can be very long, and often judges sit into the night in an attempt to hear them. Long sittings do not result in an increase in resources for family law in that circuit, so the situation continues. Despite the very best efforts of everyone concerned, the quality both of representation and of justice delivered at 8pm or 9pm must be questionable.

Further, even with such long days, sometimes cases are not reached, meaning that litigants and their legal representatives have been hanging around all day for nothing, and they must then steel themselves to go through it all again at some unspecified date months hence. Sometimes such cases involve young children, where time is of the essence and delays in a decision being made can affect the quality of their relationship with a non-custodial parent. The pressure on the lists forces judges to try to cram as many cases as possible into a day. In such circumstances it is impossible for written judgments to be given, or even for an outline to be given of the judge's reasons for making his or her orders. This does not accord with best international practice, and could be called into question by the jurisprudence of the European Court of Human Rights *(Pretto and Ors v Italy* [1984] 6 EHRR 182 and *P and B v United Kingdom* [2001] 2 FLR 261).

In other centres the court day ends promptly at 4pm or 4.30pm, sometimes even when a case is on the point of settling and being ruled, again meaning that the parties and their representatives must come back another day. It is desirable both that the court day ends at a reasonable time, and that some flexibility exists to allow cases to continue to the end if they are close to conclusion on one court day.

Judges are allocated to hear family law on a termly basis, so there is no guarantee that, if a case is adjourned (usually to the next term) the same judge will be available to hear it when it resumes. Often it is not known when a case is adjourned what the family law dates will be the following term, leaving both litigants and practitioners in uncertainty. Family law can be listed in different counties on the same circuit on the same week, meaning that practitioners working on the same circuit have difficulty in representing all their clients.

Family Law Division of Circuit Court
In the longer term there is a strong argument for a Family Law Division of the Circuit Court, staffed by judges with a special interest in or empathy for family law, and supported by ancillary services, including mediators and child welfare specialists. This proposal was made by the Law Reform Commission in 1997 and should be revisited. This need not sit in all the major county towns, but should attend the major ones and be accessible to all of them. It should sit in permanent session, supported by one or two judges and ancillary staff.

Some judges are unenthusiastic about such a change, fearing that certain judges would end up doing family law all the time, leading to a loss in expertise across the different legal disciplines. But this could be met by allocating judges to a Family Law Division for a specified period of time and rotating them. This would permit a reorganisation of the way family law lists are organised.

At the moment, a family law list will contain motions, cases that are already agreed and require ruling, and contested cases. These may not be separated in the list, so a contested case could remain in the list with little or no hope of being heard. Equally, a settled case could be waiting for hours to be ruled. A reluctant or obstructive litigant can give rise to multiple applications for furnishing particulars, orders for discovery, etc. The case will be adjourned to the next list, which could be in the next term. This pushes up the applicant's costs, as well as adding to delays. Measures are needed to reduce the opportunities for such obstruction.

Case-Management or Case-Progression

Many of these delays could be tackled by a case-management or case-progression system. A draft set of case-progression rules for family law proceedings in the Circuit Court has just been accepted by the Circuit Court Rules Committee, and legislation to facilitate this by allowing more than one County Registrar to sit currently in the same county is contained in s 30 of the Civil Law (Miscellaneous Provisions) Act 2008. Before the finalisation of these rules a pilot project was undertaken in two counties, where the County Registrars arranged for the parties' solicitors to meet with him or her informally one or more times before the case was listed in order to isolate the issues (see *Family Law Matters,* Issue 1, Number 3, for a description of the pilot project in Limerick). Issues like the valuation of the family home can frequently be agreed at this stage. Other issues, like what Discovery is required, the vouching of affidavits of means, etc., can also be agreed. If necessary, the case can come before the County Registrars' court to deal with these issues, as the County Registrar can make a number of orders relating to property matters under the Courts and Court Officers Act 2002. When a case does come up for hearing before the judge, the issues are then limited and the time wasted on Discovery and similar matters eliminated. Indeed, given that the parties and their legal representatives have an opportunity to discuss the issues in the informal forum of the County Registrar's office, some cases get settled and, if children are not involved, the County Registrar can make orders concerning settlements.

If cases were taken out of the system by mediation, by the use of collaborative law, by consents being ruled at special sittings, and then if the contested issues were defined through case-management, delays and obstruction could be reduced and judges' time could be freed up to deal with the genuinely contentious cases. Such cases could receive full consideration, and, where appropriate, written judgments could be delivered. These could then be centrally filed and edited, so that judges would have access to their colleagues' thinking on the various issues that arise in family law, thus permitting more consistency to develop.

Most of these proposals were made by the author in the Recommendations of the *Family Law Reporting Pilot Project: Report to the Board of the Courts Service* (Coulter, 2007: 61–64) and were accepted by the Courts Service Board, which has set up a sub-committee to consider the implementation of those that fall under its remit.

Children

In relation to children, no framework exists for obtaining their views regarding their own future living arrangements, education and welfare. Nor is there any training for judges on how to assess the views of children in a family dispute situation. Some judges meet the children in their chambers and talk to them, either with or without the presence of the Registrar. Others do not do so, suspecting that the children may be manipulated by one parent and not wishing to involve them in the dispute. Some judges seek a section 47 report from a child psychologist to assist them. These are normally private practitioners, and their fees may be beyond the means of some families. Alternatively, one of the parties can delay the proceedings at any stage during the case by seeking a section 47 report, or asking the HSE to prepare a "section 20 report".

There are often long delays in obtaining the services of a professional to prepare a report, and they can be expensive. More delays and additional costs can thus be added to the process. Further, there appear to be different practices in different courts about access to section 47 reports, with them being made available to the solicitors for the parties by some judges, but held to be restricted to the court itself by others.

In the past the Probation and Welfare Service offered some service to the courts of assessing children involved in family conflict, and offering guidance to the courts about their welfare. The social workers involved were able to see the children in their home, and talk to teachers and members of the Garda Síochána, if required. This service has been widely praised by court staff, judges and practitioners, but, due to under-resourcing, it had to be discontinued by the Probation Service.

There is a strong argument for re-visiting this service, and for providing a comprehensive court-based service, staffed by experienced and appropriately-trained social personnel, for assessing the needs and welfare of children in a family dispute situation. This should not depend on the ability of the parties to pay; the costs could be assessed at the end of the proceedings. Such a service should be available at an early stage, so that couples opting for mediation or for settling their case through collaborative law could avail of this expertise. Since the commencement of this research, such a service has resumed on a pilot basis in Dublin, to assist the Circuit Court.

Self-Representation

There are an increasing number of lay litigants appearing before the family law courts. While they are normally treated with care and courtesy, different judges devote different amounts of time to explaining procedures and assisting them in explaining their case. Court staff also help them as best they can, but neither they nor the judge can offer legal advice.

The dangers of self-representation are manifold. Without legal representation a person cannot be advised what to expect from litigation, or what is provided for in family law litigation, and his or her expectations of the proceedings might be unrealistic. The personal litigant may not be able to define his or her requirements and rights under the legislation, or articulate them in court. If a dependent spouse has qualified for legal aid, as he or she might, this will lead to an inequality of arms and exacerbate the litigant's frustration with the system. According to a Family Court of Australia report, self-representation may also increase opportunities for delay, reduce settlement opportunities, exacerbate hostility between the parties and lead to a reluctance to comply with orders (Family Court of Australia, 2007: 5).

All lay litigants, in both the District and the Circuit Court, should receive a standard information booklet on what to expect in court, and the eligibility criteria and charges for legal aid should be reviewed. Where there is an issue in dispute between the parties, they need legal representation. However, this may be beyond the means of some litigants. If the processing of a fairly uncomplicated judicial separation or a divorce costs €5,000–€15,000, a person earning the average industrial wage of €31,000 a year, for example, or the average salary of a public servant of €45,000, would find it very difficult to afford legal representation. They are also likely to be above the threshold for legal aid, currently set at €18,000. While allowances for accommodation, dependent spouses and children and child-care could bring that up to about €37,000, many people do not qualify for the full allowances, and if they do they have very little disposable income. They have no alternative but to seek to represent themselves.

> "Self-representation is a right. However, the right to be meaningfully heard, the nature of the adversarial system, the need for a legal system which operates efficiently, and the need to redress any power imbalance that may exist in a family relationship, are all arguments in favour of representation by an objective and skilled advocate." (Family Court of Australia, 2007: 23).

Legal Aid

There is a strong argument for removing the income limit or increasing the eligibility limit for legal aid, while asking those who become eligible and who have higher incomes to make a realistic contribution to its cost. At the moment those obtaining legal aid can be asked to make contributions which can run to some hundreds of euros. If the eligibility limit was removed or increased to, say, €50,000 a year after deductions and allowances, along with a graduated level of contribution, legal representation would become affordable to many of those at present excluded. The cost could be met by charging those at the top level of eligibility €4,000–€5,000, depending on the complexity of the case. This is what the Legal Aid Board pays to the solicitor and barrister taking a legal aid case on the private practitioners' scheme. This could only be done, of course, if the resources to the Legal Aid Board, in the form of full-time staff, were increased. But the increased fees would make the change cost-effective.

CONCLUSION

In general, the family law system can be seen to have developed in an *ad hoc* manner, with no over-arching philosophy, no statement of policy from Government as to what the objectives of the system are, no integration between its different components, no attempt to link the court system with the FMS and other forms of alternative dispute resolution, and no legislative attempt to distinguish family law from other types of litigation. The Courts Service has made a practical distinction, by trying, insofar as possible, to ensure that family law cases are heard separately from other cases. Piecemeal reform (for example, of the *in camera* rule in the Civil Liability and Courts Act 2004) has been the order of the day. Reforms such as those recommended by the Working Group on a Courts Commission (1999) and the Law Reform Commission (1996), especially where they might have involved the allocation of resources, were ignored by successive governments.

However, there are signs that this may be changing. The tenth anniversary of the enactment of the Family Law (Divorce) Act 1996 has prompted the publication of books and articles assessing where family law now stands, of which the best example is that of Geoffrey Shannon (2007). The Courts Service Family Law Reporting Pilot Project, which is continuing with the regular publication of *Family Law Matters*, produces concrete examples of what is happening in the family law courts, thus permitting more informed debate. The former Minister for Justice, Equality and Law Reform, Brian Lenihan, indicated his desire to follow up on many of the proposed reforms from the report of this project and the recommendations in Mr Shannon's book, which Brian Lenihan himself launched, though he was by then the Minister for Finance. It is to be hoped that his successor will embrace this project with equal enthusiasm, though at the time of writing he is only in office a few weeks.

The proposals contained in this work are not, therefore, either the first or the only such proposals for reform of the family law system. They are, however, based on observations of how it works in practice and it is hoped that they will supplement and enhance those made by my distinguished predecessors.

REFERENCES

Agar, M., 1980, *The Professional Stranger: An Informal Introduction to Ethnography* (London: Academic Press)

Bates, F., 1980, "The Family and Society: Reality and Myth," 15 *Irish Jurist* 195.

Binchy, W., 1984, *A Casebook on Family Law* (Abingdon: Oxon, Professional Books)

Clough, P. and Nutbrown, C., 2002, *A Student's Guide to Methodology* (London: Sage Publications)

Colgan McCarthy, I. (ed.), 1995, *Irish Family Studies, Selected Papers* (Dublin: Family Studies Centre, UCD)

Conneely, S., 2002, *Family Mediation in Ireland* (Aldershot: Ashgate Dartmouth)

Constitution of Ireland (Dublin: Government Publications Office)

Constitution Review Group, 1996, *Report* (Dublin: Government Publications Office)

Coulter, C. (ed.), (a) 2007, *Family Law Matters*, Vol. 1, No 1, Spring 2007; Vol. 1 No 2, Summer 2007; Vol. 1, No 3, Autumn 2007 (Dublin: Courts Service)

Coulter, C., (b) 2007, *Report, Family Law Reporting Pilot Project* (Dublin: Courts Service)

Courts Service, 2002, Report of the Family Law Monitoring Committee on the commencement, implementation and development of the Family Law Reporting Service Pilot Project (unpublished)

Courts Service, 2006, *Annual Report*, Courts Service (Dublin: Courts Service)

Cretney, S., 2003, *Family Law in the Twentieth Century: A History* (Oxford: Oxford University Press)

CSO, 2006, *Women and Men in Ireland 2006* (Dublin: Stationery Office)

Denham, J., 1998, *Sixth Report* Working Group on a Courts Commission (Dublin: Courts Service)

Denzin, N. and Lincoln, Y. (eds), 2005, *The Sage Handbook of Qualitative Research* (3rd edn, Thousand Oaks, California: Sage Publications)

Dewar, J. and Parker, S., 1992, *Law and the Family* (London: Butterworths)

Dewar, J., 1996, "Family, Law and Theory", *Oxford Journal of Legal Studies* 16

Dewar, J., 1998, "The Normal Chaos of Family Law", in *Modern Law Review* 61, No 4, July 1998, pp 487–485

Dewar, J. and Parker, S. (eds), 2003, *Family Law: Processes, Practices and Pressures: Proceedings of the 10th World Conference of the International Society of Family Law,* July 2000, Brisbane, Australia (Oxford: Hart Publishing)

Diduck, A., 2003, *Law's Families* (London: Lexis Nexis/Butterworths)

Diduck, A. and Kaganas, F., 2006, *Family Law, Gender and the State: Text, Cases and Materials* (2nd edn, Oxford: Hart Publishing)

Duncan, W., 1978, "Supporting the Institution of the Family in Ireland", 13 *Irish Jurist*, 215

Duncan, W.R. and Scully, P., 1990, *Marital Breakdown in Ireland: Law and Practice* (Dublin: Butterworths)

Durcan, Gerry SC, 2007, "Divorce and Judicial Separation: Recent Developments in the Superior Courts," in papers of the Thomson Round Hall's Annual Family Law Conference, 2007, November 24, 2007 (unpublished)

Eekelaar, J., 1978, *Family Law and Social Policy* (London: Weidenfeld and Nicholson)

Eekelaar, J., 1984, *Family Law and Social Policy* (2nd edn, London: Weidenfeld and Nicholson)

Fahey, T. and Lyons, M., 1995, *Marital Breakdown and Family Law in Ireland* (Dublin, Oak Tree Press)

Family Court of Australia, 2007, *Finding a Better Way* (Canberra: Family Court)

Family Support Agency, 2006, *Annual Report 2006* (Dublin: Family Support Agency)

Freeman, M.D.A., 1985, "Towards a Critical Theory of Family Law", *Current Legal Problems*, Vol 38, 1985

Glendon, M., 1977, *State, Law and Family: Family law in transition in the United States and Western Europe* (Amsterdam and New York: North-Holland Publishing Company)

Glendon, M., 1981, *The New Family and the New Property* (Toronto: Butterworths)

Harding, S. (ed.), 1987, *Feminism and Methodology: Social Science Issues* (Milton Keynes: Open University Press)

Law Reform Commission, 1996, *Report on the Family Courts* (LRC 52-1996) (Dublin: Law Reform Commission)

Law Reform Commission, 2008, *Consultation Paper on Alternative Dispute Resolution* (LRC CP 50-2008) (Dublin: Law Reform Commission)

Lee, F.R., 1996, "Influential Study on Divorce's Impact is said to be Flawed", *New York Times*, May 9, 1996

Legal Aid Board, 2006, *Annual Report 2006* (Dublin and Cahirciveen: Legal Aid Board)

McCormack, B., 2000, "Otherwise than in Public", paper on *in camera* rule to Parental Equality Conference October 2000, (unpublished)

McDowell, M., 2007, "Address by An Tánaiste at the official presentation of the Report of the Family Law Reporting Service 'Family Law Matters' at Green Street Courthouse", February 19, 2007. http://www.justice.ie/en/JELR/Pages/Speech_family_law_matters

Martin, F., 1998 "Judicial Discretion in Family Law" in 16 I.L.T. 168–174

McGinnity, F. and Russell, H., 2008, *Gender Inequalities in Time Use* (Dublin: The Equality Authority and ESRI)

Miller, G. *et al*, 2004, "Using Qualitative data and analysis: Reflections on Organisational Research, in Silverman, D. (ed.), *Qualitative Research: Theory and Practice,* (2nd edn, London: Sage Publications)

Miller, R. and Brewer, J., 2003, *The A-Z of Social Research: A Dictionary of Key Social Science Research Concepts,* (London, Sage Publications)

Nestor, J., 2003, *An Introduction to Irish Family Law* (2nd edn, Dublin: Gill and Macmillan)

Nestor, J., 2004, *Law of Child Care* (Dublin: Blackhall Publishing)

O'Brien, Carl, "Cohabiting couples the fastest-growing family unit in the Republic: *Irish Times,* October 31, 2008

O'Connor, P., 1988, *Key Issues in Irish Family Law* (Dublin: Round Hall Press)

O'Donovan, K., 1993, *Family Law Matters* (London: Pluto)

Oireachtas Committee on the Constitution, 1997, *First Progress Report* and debates, on www.constitution.ie/constitutional-reviews/apocc1997–2002.asp

Olsen, F.E., 1985 (a), "The Family and the Market: A Study of Ideology and Legal Reform," *Harvard Law Review,* Vol 96, No 7, May 1983, pp 1497–1578

Olsen, F.E., 1985 (b), "The Myth of State Intervention in the Family", *University of Michigan Journal of Law Reform,* 835

Peterson, R.R., 1996, "Statistical Errors, Faulty Conclusions, Misguided Policy: Reply to Weitzman", *American Sociological Review,* Vol 61, No 2 (June 1996), pp 539–540

Power, C., 2001, *Marital Breakdown Legislation* (Dublin: Round Hall, Sweet and Maxwell)

Power, C., 2001, *Child Law Legislation* (Dublin: Round Hall, Sweet and Maxwell)

Seale, C., 2004, *Social Research Methods: A Reader* (London: Routledge)

Shannon, G. (ed.), 1999, *The Divorce Act in Practice* (Dublin: Round Hall, Sweet and Maxwell)

Shannon, G., 2000, *The Family Law Practitioner* (Dublin: Round Hall, Sweet and Maxwell)

Shannon, G., 2001, (with Ryan, Horgan and Fennell), *Children and the Law* (Dublin: Round Hall, Sweet and Maxwell)

Shannon, G., 2002, *Family Law* (Dublin: Law Society of Ireland and Oxford: Oxford University Press)

Shannon, G., 2005, *Child Law* (Dublin: Thomson Round Hall)

Shannon, G., 2008, *Divorce Law and Practice* (Dublin: Thomson Round Hall)

Shatter, A, 1997, *Family Law* (4th edn, London and Dublin: Butterworths)

Silverman, D., (ed.), 2004, *Qualitative Research: Theory and Practice,* (2nd edn, London: Sage Publications)

Smart, C., 1984, *The Ties that Bind: Law, Marriage and the Reproduction of Patriarchal Relations* (Boston: Routledge and Kegan Paul)

Stroup, A.L., and Pollock, G.E., 1994, "Economic Consequences of Marital Dissolution", *Journal of Divorce and Remarriage,* Vol 22, Issue 1/2, 29th August 1994

Treoir, "CSO Statistics – Yearly summary", on www.treoir.ie/pdfs/BullAug07/pdf

UK Office for National Statistics, "Divorces Fall by 7 percent in 2006", www.statistics.gov.uk/cci/nugget.osp?id=170

Walls, M. and Bergin, D., 1997, *The Law of Divorce in Ireland* (Bristol: Jordans)

Walls, M. and Bergin, D., 1999, *Irish Family Legislation Handbook* Jordan's/Family Law (Bristol: Jordans)

Ward, P., 1993, *Divorce in Ireland, Who should bear the cost?* (Cork: Cork University Press)

Waters, J., 2006, "In the name of the father", *Irish Times*, August 14, 2006

Waters, J., 2006, "Families and Double Standards", *Irish Times*, May 29, 2006

Waters, J., 2006, "Silence hides the injustice", *Irish Times,* January 16, 2006

Waters, J., 2004, "Contempt for right of fathers", *Irish Times*, November 14, 2004

Waters, J., 2004, "Family courts veil injustice", *Irish Times*, October 18, 2004

Waters, J., 2001, "Why so silent if the issue is so important?" *Irish Times*, November 19, 2001

Waters, J., 2001, "Campaign by media to bury fathers", *Irish Times*, September 10, 2001

Waters, J., 1999, "Taylor's Bill still biased against fathers", *Irish Times*, May 13, 1999

Weitzman, L., 1985, *The Divorce Revolution: The Unexpected Social and Economic Consequences for Women and Children in America* (New York: Free Press)

Wood, K. and O'Shea, P., 2003, *Divorce in Ireland* (2nd edn, Dublin: Firstlaw)

Working Group on a Courts Commission, 1998, *Sixth Report: Conclusion, Summary,* (Dublin: Government Publications Office)

BIBLIOGRAPHY

Binchy, W., 1984, *Is divorce the answer?* (Dublin: Irish Academic Press)

Burgess, A. and Ruxton, S., 1996, *Men and their Children: Proposals for public policy* (London: Institute for Public Policy Research)

Byrne, A. and Leonard, M., 1997, *Women and Irish Society: A Sociological Reader* (Belfast: Beyond the Pale Publications)

Cohen, B. and Fraser, N., 1991, *Childcare in a Modern Welfare System: Towards a new national policy* (London: Institute for Public Policy Research)

Colgan McCarthy, I. (ed.), 1995, *Irish Family Studies: Selected papers* (Dublin: Family Studies Centre)

Commission on the Family, 1996 *Family Concerns: an overview of what families and the organisations who work with them had to say to the Commission on the Family* (Dublin: Commission on the Family, Department of Social and Family Affairs)

Coote, A. (ed.), 1994, *Families, Children and Crime* (London: Institute for Public Policy Research)

Duncan, W., 1982, *The Case for Divorce in the Irish Republic* (Dublin: Irish Council for Civil Liberties)

Fahey, T. and Russell, H., 2001, *Family Formation in Ireland: Trends, Data Needs and Implications,* Report to the Family Affairs Unit, Department of Social, Community and Family Affairs (Dublin: ESRI)

Galligan, Y., 1998, *Women and Politics in Contemporary Ireland: From the Margins to the Mainstream* (London and Washington: Pinter)

Hamilton, M., 1995, *The Case against Divorce* (Dublin: Lir Press)

Hewitt, P. and Leach, P., 1993, *Social Justice, Children and Families* (London: Institute for Public Policy Research)

Hug, C., 1999, *The Politics of Sexual Morality in Ireland* (Basingstoke and London: Macmillan)

Kennedy, F., 2001, *Cottage to Creche: Family Change in Ireland* (Dublin: Institute of Public Administration)

Kremer, J. and Montgomery, 1993, *Women's Working Lives,* Equal Opportunities Commission (Belfast: HMSO)

Little, J.A., 1995, *The Ban on Divorce* (Mullingar: Ennell Press)

McCashin, A., 1996, *Lone Mothers in Ireland: A Local Study* (Dublin: Oak Tree Press)

O'Connor, P., 1998, *Emerging Voices: Women in Contemporary Irish Society* (Dublin: Institute of Public Administration)

Public Policy Institute of Ireland, 1995, (a) *Women Scorned: A Response to the Second Commission on the Status of Women* (Dublin: Public Policy Institute of Ireland)

Public Policy Institute of Ireland, 1995, (b) *The Costly Consequences of Divorce: Some Salient Points* (Dublin: Public Policy Institute of Ireland)

Russell, H., Smyth, E., Lyons, M. and O'Connell, P., 2002, *"Getting out of the house": Women returning to employment, education and training* (Dublin: ESRI)

Second Commission on the Status of Women, 1993, *Report* (Dublin: Government Publications Office)

APPENDIX

COURT SERVICE PROTOCOL FOR FAMILY LAW REPORTING

1. The reports shall be published in the first instance by the Courts Service in a printed or electronic form which will be made available to the public through the media, the Courts Service website and appropriate professional publications. The Courts Service will permit its dissemination through the republication of articles and reports appearing in this publication on such terms as to identification of the source and subject to such restrictions as to re-editing as the Courts Service may specify.

2. The reporter shall take the utmost care to ensure that the reports do not contain any information that could lead to the identification of any party to the proceedings or any child involved in the proceedings. The following measures will be taken to ensure the anonymity of the parties:

   (i)   There shall be no use of the initials of the parties' names in identifying the case for the courts themselves, their staff and practitioners. Instead, reports should refer to, for example, "the applicant wife (or husband)" at first reference and "the wife" subsequently; and "the respondent husband (or wife)" and "the husband" subsequently. Where unmarried parents of children are involved, they should be referred to as "the father" and "the mother". Obviously the children should not be named, though fictional names or initials (identified as fictional) may have to be used to distinguish one from another;

   (ii) Cases reported will be given an identifier which will not include the initials of the names of the parties concerned;

   (iii) There shall be no reference to the city or town where the parties live outside Dublin and Cork, where there is a large volume of family law and courts sit almost permanently. Instead general terms such as "a provincial city" or "a town" should be used. District and Circuit Courts and judges will not be identified where this would result in the identification of the parties;

   (iv) Property will be described in general terms, for example "a substantial farm", rather than "a farm of x acres", or "a medium-sized business" rather than "a clothes shop". In certain cases involving substantial resources, however, division of these resources may account for a significant part of the judgment and be of significance in it and should be reported;

   (v)   There shall be no specific reference to a person's trade or profession unless it is relevant to the proceedings;

    (vi)   There shall be no identification of the children's school. Where the fact that they are attending a fee-paying school is relevant, it would be sufficient to refer only to "a fee-paying school" or "a boarding school abroad";

    (vii) Particular sensitivity shall be shown in dealing with psychological and welfare reports on children. Again, there may be circumstances when specific details of physical or sexual abuse should be mentioned as they would be relevant in the context of custody and access disputes, and would feature prominently in the judgment. The practice of the reporting of rape and sexual abuse cases by the responsible media offers useful experience here.

3.   Matters which are aired in the pleadings should not form part of the report unless they are opened in evidence, and/or have a bearing on the outcome of the case.

4.   The guidelines on the preservation of anonymity listed under paragraph 2 above will apply to the contents of any pleading or document filed or produced to the court in the case concerned, and to any order made therein (including the contents of any settlement ruled by the court, or produced to the court for any other purpose).

List of Author's Related Publications

1997, "Hello Divorce, Goodbye Daddy": Women Gender and the Divorce Debate, in Bradley, A. and Valiulis, M. (eds), *Gender and Sexuality in Modern Ireland* (Amherst: University of Massachusetts Press)

(a) 2007, *Family Law Matters*, Vol 1, No 1, Spring 2007, No 2, Summer 2007, and No 3, Autumn, 2007, Dublin, Courts Service

(b) 2007, *Report, Family Law Reporting Pilot Project,* Dublin, Courts Service

Index